Write
to Discover
Yourself

RUTH VAUGHN

A DOUBLEDAY-GALILEE ORIGINAL
Doubleday & Company, Inc., Garden City, New York   1980

Permission to quote material from the following sources is gratefully acknowledged:

Selections by Richard Hudnut from *Surprised by God,* copyright © 1967, Follett Publishing Company, A Division of Follett Corporation. Used by permission.

Roseanne Bergantine Giencke for her poem "Winter Is . . .", published by *Ideals.* Vol. 28, No. 6. November 1971, Christmas Ideals. Used by permission of author.

Haiku, (page 64) by Moritake, translated by Babette Deutsch from *Poetry Handbook,* fourth edition, by Babette Deutsch (Funk & Wagnalls). Copyright © 1957, 1962, 1969, 1974 by Babette Deutsch. Reprinted by permission of Harper & Row, Publishers, Inc.

Lines from "Patterns" reprinted from *The Complete Poetical Works of Amy Lowell,* copyright © 1955 by Houghton Mifflin Company. Used by permission of publisher.

"Growth" reprinted from *Walking with the Wind* by Sallie Chesham. Copyright © 1969 by Word Incorporated. Used by permission of Word Books.

"Christian Imagination" by Clyde S. Kilby reprinted from *Christian Herald* magazine. Copyright © 1979 by Christian Herald. Used by permission.

"I Believe" by Jill Hurley reprinted from *Decision* magazine. Copyright © 1970 by The Billy Graham Evangelistic Association. Used by permission.

FOR BILL
Who Was There
CARING
Through All The Agony
and The Ecstasy
Of My Own Discovery

CONTENTS

INTRODUCTION

To be asked to write an introduction is not a new experience for an author, who, like myself, has been at the business of writing books for over a quarter of a century. What is new here is that for the first time *I have asked* for the privilege. I wanted to write the introductory lines for Ruth Vaughn's *Write to Discover Yourself*.

Edmund Fuller's superior book, *Books with Men Behind Them*, has been one of my literary "bibles" for many years. He wrote it in the now-vanished period when "men" meant mankind as a whole. Indeed, the fine American novelist, Gladys Schmidt, is included. Its thrust is from Emerson's dictum: "Talent alone cannot make a writer. There must be a man behind the book" . . . an aware, sensitive human spirit to guide the words, to give them content.

Ruth Vaughn, as an author, brings Fuller's treatise sharply to mind. We have never met, but from her other writings, from her letters over the years, I know her to be a strong, believing, creative, and exuberant person. Her incredibly alive spirit spans not only the miles between us, but the even wider chasms of our differing backgrounds. Ruth Vaughn is, according to all medical wisdom, ill—housebound for the remainder of her life on earth.

Ruth Vaughn—bound?

A contradiction.

She flies.

Ruth is "behind" her book—her spirit winging, freeing mine,

freeing the bound spirits of all who read. And Heaven knows writers need to have the knots loosed.

I have written and published twenty-six books and at this writing, at least, they are all still in print. The hours I have spent in reading *this unique book on writing* have so fired me to improve my own, to give it more thought, more care, more of my short supply of patience—more old-fashioned love and devotion—that I can scarcely wait to get back to the rewrite of my own current novel manuscript.

This has been my experience, in part, because the springing spirit of Ruth Vaughn leaps from every page. There is more. Anyone, *anyone* interested in writing for any reason—from thank-you notes to poetry, to love letters, to short stories, to huge novels—can learn from the elevating and yet solid-ground practicality to be found in these pages. I doubt that anyone has been a professional too long to learn something new. For the beginning or anxious writer, for the writer with the typical "block," it is the most useful, gate-opening, mind-stirring piece I have ever read.

And it is simple. The most experienced writing intelligence should not be insulted at all; yet the young person just edging up to the muse will understand. Ms. Vaughn excludes no one. This, in itself, is quite mystifying to me. But it *is* true.

The material here has been taught, tried, and found authentic. Before her debilitating illness, Ruth Vaughn was Professor of Creative Writing at Bethany Nazarene College. But don't let that put anyone off. Every page, even the technical sections, make absorbing reading.

This is a stunningly human book and, perhaps, that is a prime value. Writers, above all people, need not only to know and take into account (and be accountable for) their own humanity, they must equally be aware of the nature of humanity around them.

I will be recommending this book for years to come to each eager, confused, frightened person—old or young—who asks me for answers about this glorious, agonizing, provocative business of writing.

I wish I had read it thirty-five years ago.

Eugenia Price
*St. Simon's Island,
Georgia*

WHATEVER YOU DO, OR DREAM YOU CAN,
BEGIN IT!

Boldness has genius, power and magic
in it.

—Goethe

1

THE INVITATION

CREATIVE WRITING IS IMPORTANT FOR ITS OWN SAKE. Every person senses flowing within him billions of vaguely understood concepts, vaguely developed perceptions, vaguely felt emotions, vaguely visible visions, vaguely internalized melodies of word patterns, vaguely evolving experiences of imagination. The person who permits this wealth of life dimensions to trip carelessly through the blur of his awareness will lose them in the maze of current impulses, superficial activity, and the focus on externals.

THE WRITER is the person willing to open all the doors of his heart, to fling wide the windows of perception, to welcome all this richness into personal experience!

THE WRITER is the person who grabs the fleeting ideas, pulls them from midair, and takes the time to analyze them until they transform into tangible reality: words written on paper to be read and reread; to be studied and restudied; to be internalized and experienced in fullest measure.

By this act, the writer has created enduring concepts from passing thoughts . . . reality from fancy . . . known from the unknown . . . understanding from the incomprehensible. And, in the doing, the writer structures for his person the record of the total blending of mind and heart. For, until that time, so much of *who he is* has flitted about in a fleeting, blurred, embryonic form.

I am convinced that writing creatively is a beautiful and rewarding experience *for discovering one's self*. For writing is one of the most forceful ways of learning, perceiving, maturing, expanding. The writer can never remain the same, for each time he takes pen in hand, he enters mentally and emotionally into the arena of transforming indefinable feelings *into* articulated definable reality. When he captures in words his inner world, he is able to add a dimension to his discernment of *self*.

I am convinced that writing creatively is a beautiful and effective worship for *one's God*. Through developing the skill to articulate one's inner impressions and understandings, one can better form an indestructible relationship with the Divine. Reeling out emotions, tangibly grappling, in words, with logic, searching to articulate personal faith enables a foundation of realism to be built which will hold firmly through all of life. And certainly, as did the Psalmist David, writing creatively our praises, our pleadings, our petitions to God enhance our worship and our trust. When the God/man dialogue is captured in black and white, the writer is able to add a dimension to his relationship with *his God*.

I am convinced that writing creatively is a beautiful and powerful service for *others*. Through sharing laughter and tears, sunshine and storm, hilarity and heartthrob from one's personal experience, we give our finest gift to those who touch our lives.

When my husband became critically ill in 1969, my wistful, fearful, loving heart wrote poetry on napkins, newspaper margins, and envelopes. Later, I retyped that torrent of emotions and had it bound into a book entitled *Silhouette of a Storm*. When he opened its pages and began to read my memories, my prayers, my lifetime promises poured out in the crisis of that illness, he wept. We clung together, caught in a tidal wave of love that made a moment-never-to-be-forgotten. My writing was important to my husband and it enhanced our marriage, enriched our love, enwrapped our lives with magic.

When caring can be captured in words, a writer is able to add a dimension to his relationship with *others*.

Because I am so firmly convinced that many need writing help, writing challenge, writing inspiration *in their own lives, for their own self-discovery,* I have written this manuscript in a warm, chatty style, inviting anyone who yearns to write out their inner feelings, their throbbing thoughts, their evolving philosophies to do just that! I have tried to avoid all formal academic language. I have striven to make this manuscript a bit like "chats over coffee" with any person seeking creative release.

I welcome the reader to spend some time with me pondering on the ways that writing creatively could help you discover your real person. Even if you never get beyond the first assignment, I am convinced that your life will be personally enriched and all your interpersonal relationships will be enhanced. This invitation could change the entire texture of your life.

Now I know many people believe that writing creatively is a skill that should be developed *only* by those who plan to make their living at publishing books and plays. This is no more true than the fallacy that no one should develop the ability to play the piano unless one plans to be church pianist or perform in Carnegie Hall. *Creative writing,* as is music, *is valuable* whether one word ever reaches print!

Perhaps I can support my thesis best in personal terms.

I have written prolifically for *God* and for *myself* since second grade. My mother preserved that first notebook of awkwardly scrawled attempts to capture in words the somersaulting feelings I had of being seven years old with my first pair of stilts!

My first effort to write for *others* was a portrait of my father lovingly created for his birthday. I was fifteen and the man I loved most in all the world read my manuscript, and cried. I knew, then, I wanted to increase my writing efforts to include those about me.

I did, ultimately, publish my work. At age twenty-one, I sold my first article. At age twenty-two, I sold my first book. And I have published more than a book a year since that time. But whether I had ever published or not, I would still spend a great deal of my time writing creatively for me, for God, for others. In diaries, journals, and notebooks, I would record life in a private, openhearted way for me, for God. In letters, personal sketches, essays, I would share my life findings with others, for God. Publishing expands one's impact just as playing in Carnegie Hall expands one's ministry to self, God, and others. But it is not vital to the qualitative value of the writing.

When I was thirty-seven, I became very ill. There followed a two-year search for a diagnosis which was made just in time to save my life. After literally being "resurrected" with the insurging flow of essential medication, my spirit exulted in joyful crescendoes. It was an exhilarating experience. As soon as strength returned sufficiently for me to write, I wheedled the essentials from an understanding nurse and began to fill pad after pad with my rioting emotions, my deepened perceptions, my gratitude for life and love, beauty and God.

One evening, I sat cross-legged on the bed looking out the seventh-floor hospital window as the sunball began to slip behind the skyline of the city and I suddenly realized that one of my greatest gifts was creative writing! I thought back to that second-grade notebook and all the way through the myriads of following notebooks, diaries, journals, detailed letters in which my heart had found its expression in the wide range of experiences I had known from age seven to thirty-nine.

On an impulse, I grabbed my pen and pad. I tried, that evening in the hospital, to articulate WHY I WRITE. Perhaps my reason will be important to you.

> I write . . .
> Not only to preserve
> The Life-venture
> But
> To revel
> In its experience
>
> . . .
> To enhance
> Its reality
> . . .
> To understand
> Its viability
> . . .
> To project it
> Into higher-sensory
> Dimensions
> Than can be seen

In the fleeting moments
Of real life.

For, to me,
A Life-venture
Is not complete
. . .
Not totally internalized
Unless
Captured in words
Made Tangible
And shared
With another.

I write . . .
To leave a personal chronicle
Logging the
Twisting, Turning
Route of my journey
For others
Who will follow.

I write . . .

To share my Inner Self
With God
And thus
Be open
To His teaching me
Deeper Truths.

Creative writing is valuable for its own sake. It will broaden, deepen, intensify your relationship with *yourself*. It can be your most vital, viable release; recording; refiner of life's experiences.

Creative writing is valuable for its own sake. It will broaden, deepen, intensify your relationship with *your God*. It can be your most vital, viable, examining experience; exulting in worship and wonder.

Creative writing is valuable for its own sake. It will broaden, deepen, intensify your relationship with *others*. It can be your most vital, viable way of saying: "I care about you!" "Let's heart-share!" "Learn from me!" "I LOVE YOU!"

I challenge you to enter this door to one of life's most exciting adventures.

Come with me.

Discover Yourself. Become a *writer!*

2

THE DIARY/JOURNAL

Direct your eye right inward, and you'll find
a thousand regions in your mind
Yet undiscovered. Travel them, and be
Expert in Home-cosmography.

Henry David Thoreau

That is the first imperative of writing creatively. You must become "Expert in Home-cosmography."

All writing, in a sense, is autobiographical. It is impossible to write unless you *know yourself* and are willing to attempt to identify, portrait, and explain *who you are* in words.

When I taught creative writing in college, I used to write two words on the board for the students' first assignment. They were:

I WHY?

I offer you that question as your first and ever-ongoing assignment in writing creatively. Get yourself a notebook or diary (often called by writers "The Journal") in which you write those two words at the top or center of page one. The rest of that book, and all the other notebooks you will fill as diary/Journals, will be answer to that query.

You must know *who* you are, but to find that answer, you must first understand *why* you are!

When I was in college, I could have glibly rattled off an answer to *who* I was. Now, as an adult looking back through all of my life carefully, I come to a perception of *why* I was that girl in college . . . and it changes the glib answer I would have given of *who* I was.

So I am asking that, in your diary/Journal, you begin a journey through your life. Try to capture in words your parents'
physical appearances
their personalities
your feelings for them . . . your relationship.

Strive to be as explicit and detailed as you can be.

One of my students wrote me this note when first confronted with this assignment:

> The drawback is that I'm afraid to look into my own experience and my emotions because I don't want to reveal that much of me. I know a Journal is a private thing which should not be available for any eyes than mine . . . yet putting into words all my inner feelings, dreams, relationships . . . fears, frustrations, failure . . . demands a personal revelation that I don't know if I'm ready to meet.

She was right. A diary/Journal does make the kind of demand for personal honesty that you may have avoided before. But if you really desire to live life to its fullest . . .
desire to write creatively for self, for God, for others . . .
you *must* be willing to become "Expert in Home-cosmography."

Begin by trying to "portrait" the important people in your life. In an effort to describe my father, I wrote these words:

> My father's face shows kindness as some men's show vice and greed. His voice is rich and deep, like a river stretching out into the ocean. And as a child, when I listened to him read the part in the New Testament about love, the house was full of music. It wasn't just his enunciation that was good; it was the spirit in him that seemed to kindle a flame in the fine words.

He is a big man with wide shoulders and strong arms. I was six years old before I knew that the Bible was speaking of God rather than my father when it referred to the "everlasting arms." I heard it often and I always snuggled inside because I knew exactly how those arms felt. Every night, he'd grab me to his heart, fling me in the air, pull me back to safety, brush his lips across my cheek and then "the everlasting arms" would carry me to bed!

In my father lives a splendid simplicity and an unshakable honesty. You can always find him over there in the Sermon on the Mount, doing unto others as he desires them to do unto him.

There is no sophistry about this man. There is a power of plain goodness and kindness which shows in him like a campfire on a dark night. It is as warm as a campfire too.

One of my friends allowed me to take this excerpt, describing her father, from the beginning of her Journal when we were in college together:

He was as thin as a stick man. His clothes hung on him like a scarecrow's. Although he bought expensive clothes, they always sagged on his emaciated frame. His face was lined with the scars of broken commandments. His smile was mocking and when his face was serious, his lips formed a cruel line.

His eyes were the most frightening. They appraised me often as a hunter would look at his quarry. I've never been hunting or seen the look in a hunter's eyes, but I'm sure I'm correct in the analogy because I *was,* indeed, his quarry. He tripped me for the fun of seeing me fall. He would offer me a cookie to get me close enough to slap. And when he was angry, I was the release-valve of his emotions. The imprint of his fists still mark my body.

In reading these brief excerpts from two persons trying to "portrait" their father, do you see why such an endeavor is of benefit to the person hoping to become "Expert in Home-cosmography?" From these scant paragraphs, you, the reader, can quickly gain

an idea of *why* I would become *who I am* . . . and *why* my
friend would become *who she is!*

Just as did we.

When I first attempted this assignment, I began to realize
there was no way I could ever truly know and understand
myself without knowing and understanding my father and my
mother and the effect their lives and our relationship had in
molding me.

The same was true for my friend . . . but much more startling.

After she had written the above paragraphs, she called me on
the phone and said: "After putting the elusive memory of my
father (he died when I was eight) into words that are tangible,
graphic reality, I have already come to an understanding of some
of my starkest terrors."

In your diary/Journal, strive to bring to "tangible, graphic
reality" the people important in your early life: parents, siblings,
other family members, neighbors, friends, and enemies. Try to
"portrait" your personal image of each in the detail that is true
for you!

My friend's father was declared "Jaycee of the Year" before he
died. The "portrait" written by a news reporter in his obituary
would have no place in his child's diary/Journal. The public young
leader has no relevance in the relationship between a frustrated
man seeking a "release-valve for his emotions" on his tiny
daughter.

There are intangible personalities in our lives that also may
need to be captured in "tangible, graphic reality" as they existed
in your early life. I speak of such things as Poverty . . . Wealth
. . . "The Other Side of the Tracks" . . . "The High IQ" . . .
Physical Impairments . . . Physical Prowess, et cetera. These intangible, but pervasive, specters also were formative and need
exploration in your becoming "Expert in Home-cosmography."

After striving to honestly draw word pictures of these influences
in your life, begin to journey back in memory to your earliest
experiences. Take the time to write out as specifically as possible
the things you remember. Times you laughed. Times you cried.
Times you spent in the top of your mulberry tree (or wherever

was your "secret place" in childhood). Times at school when you
were a success. Times socially when you were a failure.

Probe.

Remember.

Write it out.

Let no experience be too insignificant to try to recapture.

In perusing experiences, stilts came to my mind. I had not
thought of such things in years. (Does anyone walk on stilts today?
I never see them! Pity! It *was* great fun!) I was five when I
learned to walk on stilts that were low to the ground; I was six
when I learned to walk on my brother's tall stilts. (End of story.)

No point in writing *that* in my diary/Journal . . . right?

But . . . since it was an experience that came to mind, I decided to go ahead and put it down. As I wrote about it, I was reminded of how my brother made fun of me that first year of our
stilt-walking adventures because I wouldn't try his stilts. I'd get on
the porch balcony, take the tall ones in hand, look them over and
then let them fall to the ground. Laugh as he would, my brother
could not goad me into trying his stilts.

One day my father was observing the futility of my brother's
efforts to get me to leave my short stilts. He said: "Leave her
alone. When her body's ready for higher stilts, she'll know! Till
then, she has no business trying."

Sure enough, the next spring I got out my brother's stilts,
climbed up to the porch balcony, stepped into the stirrups, and
walked away. I wobbled, but I walked. My body's inner timing
knew I was ready.

And in that brief exploration of a trivial incident that had totally slipped my mind, I remembered words of my father that
have held me steady in a lot of life's seasons. When utterly terrified
about something, I remember his words about one's own inner
wisdom and I step aside. I proved with the stilts . . . and have
proved through the years since . . . that when I am inwardly
ready for a task, I will know. There may be fear, but not
abject terror.

I am asking that you take the time and effort to go back and
try to capture the memories of your life from earliest childhood
to the present. Let nothing be too trivial to explore. If it survives
in your memory, it was significant in some way.

From such inner exploration will come self-knowledge, life-understanding, and increasing dimensions of wisdom. . . . Also, you will be forming a reservoir of material which will provide the "stuff" of your writing in all future years. Whether you want to write an essay, a poem, a drama, or a story, its general essence will come from what you learn in your diary/Journal. Often its specific expression will come from the record of your personal journey.

Now.

I hope you are beginning to understand the value of the diary/Journal for a person who would write creatively.

But, there is another facet. That is . . . that you begin, now, to discipline yourself to record life as it is now evolving for you.

Write your experiences, your emotions, your reactions in as much detail as possible. Later you can go back and study those heart-reeling words written in the impetus of the moment of triumph or tragedy and learn for yourself . . . and be able to share with others. But now it is important to get it DOWN . . . in as much detail as possible.

A young minister, Richard K. Hudnut, did this so well that succinct pieces were excerpted from his diary/Journal and made into a book. It is called *Surprised by God*. It would be a terrific addition to your library and stimulate your own diary/Journal writing.

Let me share some of the notations he wrote in his diary/Journal as he lived through his ministerial life.

One of our officers died suddenly. That afternoon we had a special service of memory for him. That night I called a little girl to wish her "Happy Birthday." What is extraordinary about this job is that it keeps you in touch with birth and death, love and hate, joy and sorrow. When a baby is born, you are there. When a man dies, you are there. When a man and woman want to live the rest of their lives together, they come to you. When they are fed up, they come back to you. This means that a minister must be flexible. He must be able to go from death to birth in a matter of hours, or from a divorce to marriage in the swing of his door. I'm afraid I'm not always as flexible as I should be. And as I said "Happy

Birthday" to the little girl, I hope she did not hear the sadness in my voice for the death of my friend. (p. 17)

Our family ate dinner with another church family. It doesn't happen as often as you might think. When it does, I am struck with how I would like to go into every home in the church with a tape recorder (or seismograph, as the case may be). You can tell a lot about a family by the way they behave at the dinner table. Hearing themselves would be quite revealing. Think I'll run an ad in our church paper: "Pastor for Hire. Will Sit in on Family Dinner with Tape Recorder and Give Free Report of Findings." (p. 29)

She went downstairs in the morning and died across her ironing board. Twenty-seven years old. Two children. "How do you explain it?" people ask. I want someone to explain it to me. Who is going to be a pastor to me at such times? I am alone with God and no answers come and then I am expected to go out there and give answers. (p. 18)

Those excerpts give you an idea of the function of the diary/Journal: moments of life recorded in the tangible of words, preserved for all time, but I want to remind you that those excerpts came from a published book! Your diary/Journal will not sound like that. Your Journal should be the place where you can honestly scribble out all of your emotions in whatever power you are feeling that day WITH NO REGARD WHATEVER for the way the words are put together.

Because my collegians kept a diary/Journal as a part of their class requirements, they had to turn them into me so that I could know they had written in the book regularly. I promised not to read the private and precious recordings, but I had to thumb through the pages to be able to give an evaluation of how well they fulfilled the assignment.

I noted that many of them made the mistake of taking the Journal assignment so seriously in the beginning that their entries were brief, concise, every word correctly spelled, proper punctuation, et cetera. But as they grew familiar with the class and the goals of the assignment, the entries became longer, sloppier, and parts of them written in such emotional turmoil the words were incomprehensible to anyone other than their own eyes. *That* was when I smiled and knew they had begun the real journey of writing creatively.

For the greatest hurdle a beginning writer must overcome is the one he sets for himself: perfection. He approaches a Journal entry as if he had been commissioned to write the Great American Novel with a rigid command from an overbearing editor that not a single mistake would be allowed. And so superficial nonsense comes out: "See Jane run. See Skip run after Jane."

And nothing is accomplished.

My challenge to you is to approach the diary/Journal as your best friend in the world. You can pour out things here you might not dare *say* to anyone else. No one is going to ever read your diary/Journal unless you ask them to. This is not for publication in the *Reader's Digest*. This is *you* taking Thoreau's advice to "Direct your eye right inward" and travel the "thousand undiscovered regions in your mind." And for such a journey, you cannot have the *slightest* concern for correct form, neatness, or intelligibility to anyone except yourself and God. And, in later reading, some of it may be decipherable only to God . . . but that is all right! Even the illegible gives you a "feel" for the tumult of your heart at that moment. And that is a recording within itself.

Just pound out whatever comes to mind as quickly as you can. And the more you write, the better: the more release it will give you; the more insight it will provide; the more accurate will be the record when you come back later to reread and learn from it truths that will enrich self-understanding and that you may be able to share with others.

In one of my student's Journals were words so glaring I could not keep from reading them because one entire page was filled with three words printed with such fervor that the page was torn on some of the lines. The words were: I HATE LIFE! Because I knew the student well, when I returned the Journal, I explained I could not keep from reading that entry and asked if she wanted to talk about it.

She did. And she's given me permission to share that heart-ripping entry with you and its following page:

There! I've said it and I'm glad. I know my mother would be
horrified and banish me to my room if she knew such thoughts
were even in my head. But they are and now that I have
written them out in anger, I feel better. Everything's wrong
and bad and broken for me. I wish I did not have to
live. But I don't know how to get out. If I tried to wreck the
car, with my luck, I'd bruise my knee and my folks would
make me pay damages. But I'm alone and no one cares and
no one even knows I exist really. My mother is too busy to
notice anything I do; I doubt my father has ever known I was
more than another mouth to feed. WHY DOESN'T SOME-
ONE NOTICE ME? Ohhhhhhhhhhh Ohhhhhhhhhh How I
hate life! hatehatehatehatehatehate!! That's all: hatehatehate-
hatehatehatehatehatehatehate!!

And then the tears came and those pages are still warped from
the flood that fell in that dark moment. But it was *free* release
for her to write out her emotions and tipped open the floodgate
of tears that were refreshing. And she also gained a permanent
record of how it felt to be nineteen years old facing a particular
set of circumstances.

From such understanding will come wisdom that you can later
share with others . . . in letters, in gifts, and, perhaps, in print.
But first you must explicitly detail *who* you are . . . *why* you
are . . . in the past and in the ongoing formation of your
personal *who* and *why*.

The diary/Journal is invaluable.

Make it your daily companion.

Write in it with total honesty and freedom.

It will serve you well and in its pages you will soon clearly
see that writing creatively is valuable . . .

> for YOU
> for YOUR GOD
> for YOUR OTHERS.

The diary/Journal is probably *the* most important tool in your
writing creatively. From it, you can continue, through rereading
and appraisal, to learn more about yourself and God. You can see

your life as it develops and grows. You can see how your writing begins to improve, because you learn to write BY WRITING!

When I was a graduate student, I went to a seminar to listen to a famous author speak gems of wisdom to make us "instant best sellers!" When he stood to his feet, he shocked us all by saying: "So you want to be writers? What are you doing here? Why aren't you at home at the typewriter? *That* is the only place you are going to learn to write."

And he was right.

You learn to write Your Style BY WRITING!

And no one, no matter how successful he may be, can teach you how! You learn with hoursandhoursandhoursandhoursand hoursandhours spent WRITING!

Then, if that be true, why did I take degrees in creative writing and teach classes on a college campus for eight years? Indeed, why am I writing to you at all?

Because . . . another *can* inspire you to write creatively . . . another *can* give you shortcuts learned by the masters that will help you develop more quickly . . . another *can* give some technical rules that will polish your work for sharing with others.

But whether or not you write creatively is *your* choice. Because you do, indeed, learn to write BY WRITING!

A prolific writer, M. Lee Falkowski, had never done anything but dream about writing until he was fifty years of age and facing a year of recuperation following spinal surgery. He decided he would write a million words of "practice writing" before he ever submitted anything to a publisher.

And he did.

He wrote in as much detail as he could muster about the important people in his life, the experiences he could remember, and kept an account of the events and feelings of the present as he lived it *with no regard* for technical beauty. He was becoming "Expert in Home-cosmography"; he was recording the "stuff" from which all future writing would come both in the general and specific senses; *and* he was practice-writing a thousand words a day for a thousand days!

From such practice comes expertise . . . as his list of publication credits now shows.

So this is my first and, in a very real way, my most important challenge to you: If you would write creatively, begin a diary/ Journal where you write only for yourself and God. You are totally free from the English teacher's red pencil. You are working to record LIFE as it was, as it is, and thus learn the answer to the imperative question:

I WHY?

3

THE TIME

After understanding the function of the Journal . . . and sensing there may be more to come . . . you are probably shrinking back or yelling heatedly: *Where* do you think I'm going to find that kind of time?

I understand your panic so well because I faced it in both forms every semester in every class for eight years. I would never get through that Journal assignment without someone asking, either fearfully or belligerently: "Has it *ever* occurred to you that we are taking *other* classes than this one?" And the rest of the class would sigh their relief that the fact had *finally* been called to my attention.

So you are wondering *how* you could ever find "all that time" in the midst of your own pressure-packed schedule. You're already wishing for a forty-eight-hour day and a nine-day week! *How* are you going to find "free uninterrupted time" to spend on self-exploration in a Journal?

First I will say what you expect me to say: You will have to take a close look at your priorities. If you had made the choice to begin piano lessons, you would have to schedule hours of practice at the keyboard into your schedule. You know that from the outset. The same thing is applicable to the art of writing creatively. There has to be time set aside for you to "practice" . . . for you to develop your skills. And so it will have to be considered in the establishment of your priorities. The amount of time you set aside for "free uninterrupted" work is dependent upon your decisions in regard to priorities.

Now I will say what you may not have expected. You *can* become a creative writer on your schedule, no matter how harried, *if you choose to do so!* Because you see . . . time may be defined in many ways.

The author of *The Best Time of Year* and other excellent books, Irving Petite, wrote: "I do not believe in the l-o-n-g hours that some writers . . . profess to put in." And he, then, shares how he worked very hard on a ranch and had little time or energy for "free uninterrupted hours." But he said that he was always thinking, looking, perceiving, and then, late at night, he scrawled as quickly as possible his thoughts of the day. And ultimately this discipline and this record enabled him to launch into a successful career.

That sounds terrific for Mr. Petite, doesn't it? But squeezing in bits and pieces of writing doesn't sound very workable to you. You've always thought of the writer as spending "free uninterrupted hours," and that remains your image.

Well . . . let's shatter the image. First of all, note that Mr. Petite said that writers "profess" . . . to spend long hours writing! Do they really? Or is a lot of that time spent sharpening pencils, watering the ivy, examining one's navel, and daydreaming? If you really had days and days of "free uninterrupted hours," would you *really write?*

There is an old Scottish proverb that says: "What may be done at any time will be done at no time." I think that's right! Your busy schedule may truly be a blessing . . . because you have only "set times" you can write freely, uninterrupted . . . and because of that pressure, you *will* write rather than fix the crease in your slacks or bite your nails.

Also the writer has a blessing that the pianist does not. You can be at your work wherever you are, even on the run! My Journals are so messy that I have made my husband promise to burn them at the moment of my death. Not only is there pure freedom for bad writing in the Journals and sloppy typing and penmanship . . . *but* the thing that is worse is that my Journals are filled with napkins . . . torn margins from newspapers . . .

calling cards, envelopes, empty match containers from restaurants, et cetera. And I keep all that "junk" *because* each is a *part* of my Journal. In a restaurant waiting for my meal, or in the midst of it, I get an impression, an idea, and I grab a napkin or match container and jot it down. In the car, in doctor's waiting rooms, wherever I happen to be when an inspiration hits, I jot it down. A few jumbled words which make no sense to anyone else . . . but they do to me! There is an envelope on which is penned the words of a poem that, to me, is priceless. I doubt anyone else could even read the phrases . . . but I can. And when I do, I remember the exact emotions that were flooding me. That envelope transports me back to a hospital room where my husband lay dying . . . and I sat in the semidarkness huddled in a strain trying to make the next breath come for him . . . and, on impulse, I grabbed an envelope from the trash can and poured out my feelings for this beloved man of my life in words that both he and I cherish. They are now preserved in print . . . but I keep the envelope because it is *there* that the real *feel* comes!

One of my friends read the poem in a book and called me. She said: "You could never write like that again!" And it is true. Because I could never *feel* like that exactly again.

The pianist can only be at work where a weighty piano sits. But the writer can be at work all the time.

One of my favorite stories in this regard is that Johann Strauss wrote the inimitable waltz "The Beautiful Blue Danube" on his shirt sleeve. Caught in a moment of inspiration, he couldn't find an envelope, napkin, or newspaper margin . . . so he captured the notes in his head on his shirt sleeve. Busy with other things, he forgot about it and the shirt went into the laundry. Accidentally, his wife noticed it on the shirt sleeve and saved it for posterity.

That *time* for writing is yours. In the regular activities of your life, keep yourself constantly on the alert for "stuff" to write about. Much of it may be held forever in the words you scribble on the run. Some of it you will want to develop more fully when you do have hours of "free uninterrupted quiet."

For example, I was driving one day thinking of my mother and how I would like to write a detailed tribute to her. But I didn't know how to go about it. Suddenly, I got a flash: structure it on Ecclesiastes 3 and, thus, show the beauty of her life "in all seasons." I pulled to the side of the road, grabbed a map and wrote the idea and some other fleeting thoughts about it on the map, thrust the map into the car pocket and drove on home.

I forgot about the incident until I was given a class assignment in graduate school to "portrait" a personality. When class was over, I went to the car, got out the roadmap, and there was the inspiration preserved for me in detail.

Using the notes on the roadmap, I spent "free uninterrupted hours" writing a "portrait" that was later published as a book. But the idea came "on the wing" and might never have returned . . . had I not grabbed a moment in the regular schedule of my life to note it. There, preserved for me, was the idea waiting for the time I could put it to use.

Keep a notebook with you (it works better than the napkins, shirt sleeves, and roadmaps!) so that, at red lights, or in the long line at the department store, you can jot down your ideas. But when a notebook isn't handy, just "make-do" with whatever is! You don't have time to develop it then. But throw it "in" your Journal or a box for such things . . . and it is there, preserving for you the moment of inspiration . . . the fleeting embryonic emotions or perceptions.

My minister father used to say that when he had an important job to be done in the church, he asked the busiest layman to do it. The reason? That busy man knew how to schedule his time, organize, and *get things done* . . . whereas the layman "with all the time in the world" would take just *that long!* Were you miraculously freed from the demands of your world, you probably would not write much more, maybe not as much, as when you schedule your time. Now you have deadlines to motivate you.

So take a long hard look at your priorities in life. You want to write creatively? Then you will have to work in hours for pure writing in the schedule. The more the better. But it does not mean that you have to cease all other activities! You can write creatively a record "on the wing" that is both meaningful within itself . . . or will capture essence until you have time to develop it fully.

Make the most of every minute.

Writing is of such a nature that it can be a part of your every moment of every day. Writing is, indeed, a WAY OF LIFE!

4

THE TALENT

Talent is long patience. It is a question of regarding whatever one desires to express long enough and with attention close enough to discover a side which no one has seen and which has been expressed by none. In everything there is something of the unexplored, because we are accustomed to using our eyes only with the thought of what has already been said concerning the things we see. The smallest thing has in it a grain of the unknown. Discover it. In order to describe a fire that flames or a tree in the plain, we must remain face to face with that fire or that tree until for us they no longer resemble any other tree or any other fire. This is the way to become original.

—*Guy de Maupassant*

Too many people define talent as "genius" and that lets them "off the hook" because there are few who fit into that category. The definition given above is much more disturbing because it places responsibility squarely upon the individual.

I think there is some truth in the stereotype of a need for "genius" in writing. I think the "spark" of enthusiasm for searching out the meanings of life and trying to transform their intangible essence into the tangible written word must be there. And I think that you can claim that "spark" as your own simply because you have been/are in such exploration at this moment. But to allow your definition of the creative writer to be limited to Shakespeare is ridiculous . . . Or even to Erma Bombeck who keeps us laughing with her comments on life that have now broken into best-selling print.

My point, again, is that you do not have to be (now or ever . . . although you *may*) published for your writing to be important. Every line you write is a reflection of yourself, your world, your philosophy and that is important. Important to *you*. Erma's writing was delightful fun, and helped preserve her sanity, for *herself,* for finding the joy in God's world, and for others with whom she shared her work . . . even if one word had never been published. Only the *enlargement* of numbers profiting from her efforts comes from the published books and columns. They were still of *value* in the small world that really mattered to her before print.

So, at this point, don't compare yourself with a genius or even a published writer. Assume, from your own self-knowledge, that the "spark" is there or you would never have considered writing creatively. And then accept this definition of talent: It is "long patience."

One of my dear friends has had "long patience" at the piano. She has the "spark" and has practiced the necessary hours until she plays beautifully. No one has yet proclaimed her another Van Cliburn nor has she been asked to perform in Russia. But she plays for self-expression, worship and service to God in her local church, and for others who listen, in the services, in her home, and on the tapes she makes at our requests. I have records of Van Cliburn, but they remain in their jackets in the corner. The tapes of my friend's playing are on my cassette daily bringing me joy.

Music is important whether or not you ever tour the world or appear on national television in a concert. Most people recognize that fact and accept it.

Writing creatively is important whether or not you ever publish a best-seller. That is not as generally accepted. I hope you *will* publish! I believe that if you work at the development of your talent (with both definitions), you *can* publish! But I don't want you to feel that it is an imperative if you cultivate this art.

A former student wrote recently to tell me that, in the midst of diapering and feeding three babies, she still worked in her Journal. "But," she wrote despondently, "I don't know if I'll ever do anything with it!"

"Ever do anything with it!"

What a letter I wrote her!

Writing creatively is *valuable* for its own sake. That Journal record of life knee-deep in children is something she, her husband, and those growing lives will cherish always. If it is never even recopied in prettier handwriting or in more standard form, that heart-sharing is important for all those concerned.

I have Journals of my mother since she was fifteen years of age. She never published a word. She never did "anything" with her writing. But we, her children, hold these records of her life— later of our lives—sacred.

When you thoroughly internalize, you can be your freest in working where *you are now!* You don't have to be concerned about editorial opinions. The publishing may come. That, you and God will work out when the time comes. But for now . . . you are writing the free-wheeling impressions of life *as you see it* . . . and that is *valuable* within itself!

Sean O'Faolain, an Irish writer, said that what would-be writers need is "not instruction in the art of writing, but in the art of living." I believe that is most pertinent.

If you would develop your "talent," you must learn a new way of life . . . you must develop "the art of living." That comes from grinding your inner lenses to perceive things in original and transparent form. To do so is a deliberate act of your mind and will. It is difficult to view everyday sights and find much there. That is not our custom because we have spent a lifetime looking only at superficialities. We never take time or energy to focus on the specifics that compose our reality. We move in a small *known* familiar maze . . . and all else, for the most part, remains little comprehended and vaguely threatening. So, for self-safety, we stay within narrow confines and batten down the hatches of wider experience.

One of my professors said that the writer is the person with his skin off. He is openly cognizant . . . personally unlocked . . . in sensory-full contact with all experiences. He looks. He listens.

He feels. He tastes. He touches. He is sensitively *aware* of facial expressions, body nuances, communications uttered verbally and non-verbally, relationships, actions, and reactions.

Wherever you find people laughing, crying, loving, hating, succeeding, failing . . . wherever you find bulging mountains, blue skies, a tree or flower . . . wherever you personally gain a sharpened understanding of a part of life as you know it . . . there is the "stuff" that will develop your talent. You don't have to move out of the spot where you are now to write creatively! Those who insist that inspiration demands change and new vistas are in error. Those who insist that inspiration comes only at the prayed-for coming of the elusive muse are wrong. Inspiration comes, as does talent, "with long patience." Begin where you are with who you know, what you see, what you perceive.

That is why my first assignment, and perhaps the most important assignment to be made, is the Journal. Writing creatively (which really means living . . . thinking . . . observing creatively) begins with the everyday. A. A. Whitehead, the philosopher, wrote: "It requires a very unusual mind to undertake an analysis of the obvious." You must cultivate this "unusual mind." If you cannot see, touch, smell, hear, and comprehend the everyday, your writing will be sterile and austere.

As you dig into yourself, and into your known world, you will be able to write so that when you share your words, others will read with a shock of recognition: Hey! That's how I felt when . . . I just didn't know how to say it!

This requires a depth of honesty that is painful . . . but imperative. The test of good writing is the sense of truth in the manuscript: its clarity, its spontaneity, its authority. Read Balzac, Tolstoi, Faulkner, and Mauriac. You will find the everyday . . . but in the *obvious* shines out unsuspected meanings!

Schopenhauer wrote: "The first rule of good style is to have something to say . . . but how can one have something to say if one is asleep to one's experience?" The first step in the "long patience" spoken of by Guy de Maupassant is to awaken yourself to clearly perceive the significance in everything about you: the people, the atmosphere, the natural world, the concrete world, the relationships, the ideas, the books, the emotions, the events. Emily Dickinson rarely left her house, but her quickened sensitivity to the commonplace things of life made her writing inimitably rich.

I challenge you to be courageous enough to fling wide the door, open wide the windows, throw out your arms in vulnerability to the experiences of life. Let them engulf your spirit, deluge your heart. Let LIFE enter your senses and understanding full-personed. Let it invade; let it flood through; let it explode. Only the accessible soul can reach the heights of writing creatively.

The definition of talent in regard to "the spark" of genius is yours or you would have no desire to write. The definition of talent as "long patience" is the one that must concern you. To write creatively will mean hard work, much time, and a great deal of effort in learning to live, think, *and* write with meaning.

So. You are confronted with this axiom: "The spark" of talent is God's gift to you. What you do with it (the long patience required) is your gift to Him.

5

THE PRAYER

O God:

Make me responsive and impressionable so I may comprehend the significant in the commonplace.

Help me to perceive deeply and fully so that my words will enlarge and brighten my inner sphere and that of all who read.

Give me the capacity to prompt laughter when despair is prompting tears; and give me the capacity to trigger tears when self-insulation has barred out the suffering of another.

Grant me the strength to write honestly and deeply from my soul in spite of what others might think or say.

Make me vulnerable so that I may grow through suffering to a dimension where my words will be valuable to others in pain.

Help me to understand that my writing can shatter or inspire . . . my words can present a narrow view or call spirits to an expansive vision . . . my creativity has the power to blacken horizons with cynicism or irradiate the world with faith.

Give me the capacity to dare door-opening when fear is holding adventure captive; and give me the capacity to stand before God-sealed doors and hold, in loving sharing, another's hand.

Grant me the ability to write when comments about my efforts are vitriolic and my heart sags with the certainty that nothing I create is valuable to me, to You, or to anyone else. Grant me the ability to write EVEN THEN.

O God: help me to believe that writing is true to my nature and, therefore, my gift from You. I pray You will enable me to believe in my creative endeavors . . . and in myself . . . EVEN WHEN . . .

> no one else
> seems
> to believe
> in either.

Amen.

6

THE NOTEBOOK

All through my boyhood and youth, I was known and pointed out for the pattern of an idler; and yet I was always busy on my own private end, which was to learn to write. I kept always two books in my pocket, one to read, one to write in. As I walked my mind was busy fitting what I saw with appropriate words; when I sat by the roadside I would either read or a pencil and a penny version book (blank book we would call it) would be in my hand, to note down the features of the scene or commemorate some halting stanzas. Thus I lived with words. And what I thus wrote was for no ulterior use, it was written consciously for practice. It was not so much that I wished to be an author (though I wished that too) as that I vowed that I would learn to write.

—*Robert Louis Stevenson*

There is a delightful book you should read. It is called *A Room Made of Windows* written by Eleanor Cameron. (Atlantic-Little, Brown, 1971) If you open its pages, you will find a girl named Julia Redfern. Julia keeps a "Book of Strangenesses." In this book, she makes lists. Some of her lists look like this.

BEAUTIFUL WORDS: MOST DETESTABLE WORDS:
Mediterranean Rutabaga

Quiver   Larva
Undulating   Mucus
Lapis Lazuli   Okra
Empyrean

Julia craved "a desk covered with such highly desirable possessions as paper clips and rubber bands, and a stamp pad and rubber stamps, and a holder for pens and pencils, and various boxes
with cards in them, and a big blotter." And Julia's father got them
for her in spite of her grandmother's conviction that such a gift
was "a strange great thing to make for a child Julia's age."

Although other themes are present in the book, it draws a beautiful picture of a girl growing into a writer. As I read it, I kept
thinking: Yes! Of course! I did that too!

There is a universality about the nature of writers. Even if one
doesn't begin to write until the age of fifty, like Lee Falkowski
who began by writing a million words of practice before letting
an editor look at his work . . . even if the serious writing does
not begin until late in life . . . I think there are striking likenesses
in the spirit and loves of writers throughout their lives.

Malcolm Cowley propounded this thesis and proved it admira-
bly in *The Literary Situation*. He found that most professional
writers held in common such things as a love for reading, deep
feelings of loneliness or isolation at periods in their lives, need
for approval, of at least a few people, of their literary efforts.

Think back in your life.

Do you recall feelings of loneliness?

Did you love to read?

Did you make lists?

I did and so does Julia. That is why the book is so delightful to
me. And in its final pages, Julia writes in her "Book of Strangenesses":

> If I do turn out to be a writer, and a good one, I'll always be
> pulling things out of myself that I didn't know I knew and
> that I didn't know I understood. . . . I wonder if this is the
> way it's going to be! If it is, which would be exciting, but hard
> too . . . then I am surely going to be one. I wouldn't miss it
> for anything.

Neither would I.
Please . . . don't you!

All of which leads me, as you fully suspected, to the next real assignment. Again, this is a challenge to begin something that will be a part of your daily life from now on. Its purpose is different from the diary/Journal. There, you are striving for self-exploration and preservation of life's experiences. It provides you with the opportunity for full emotional release, the practice of writing as rapidly as possible, the struggle to capture every fleeting thought regardless of how roughly it is structured. The Journal is the storehouse of the essence of *who* and *why* you are and from it, you will gather "stuff" for your writing all of your life.

This assignment is for what we shall call simply "The Notebook." Its goal is to begin technical work on learning how to be a writer. It is, in fact, the same as Julia's "Book of Strangenesses" . . . the same as Robert Louis Stevenson's "blank book." This is where you stretch your brain to be as creative in *expression* as you can be.

Since Julia enjoyed lists, let's begin there.

A Notebook, to be its most effective, may contain all kinds of lists. Scott Fitzgerald, a great writer, said one of his chief manias was lists. He kept lists of popular songs of a particular year. Lists of slang phrases current in a certain era. Lists of his most pleasant trips. Lists of his most unpleasant trips. Lists of cities. Lists of cavalry leaders. Lists of football players.

I used to keep lists of all the books I had read. Lists of songs I had memorized. Lists of people I admired where each name was followed by a listing of the dominant trait that charmed me most. Lists of my favorite friends from books or make-believe.

Shirley Eclov, author of such books as *The Whipping Boy*, wrote that when she was writing a story, she made lists of characteristics about them. She would write down such things as:

what he eats for breakfast	what he wears to bed
favorite color	his attitude toward dogs
mother's maiden name	his favorite kind of ice cream
favorite clothing store	

From this list, she would gain insight into the character she was creating. Instead of just a name, suddenly a full-blown person who likes red, shops at the Salvation Army, and eats peanut-butter ice cream emerges.

You may find other kinds of lists that you think will be fun and helpful for you in your working toward becoming a writer. But there are two that I would specifically suggest.

Begin now to note in your reading . . . in your dictionary . . . in your conversation STRONG VERBS. Then take the time to write them down. It will not only increase your vocabulary but will give you a resource on which to draw in your writing. As we will discuss in more detail later, verbs constitute the strongest part of writing. One strong verb can do more in drawing a word picture than fourteen adjectives. So begin now to use your notebook for lists of *verbs*.

I picked up a short story and at random made this list.

VERBS:

Echoed	Boomed
Trembled	Twisted
Slammed	Scrambled
Hesitated	Huddled
Smashed	Crawled
Roared	Bounced
Reverberated	

As you become sensitive to verbs for your list-making, and actually write them out, your writing will become more and more verb-oriented which is an important strength.

The second list I strongly advise is a list of effective phrases used in description. Again, this will make you aware of the power of such word pictures in your reading, conversations, and television viewing. Taking the time to write them down will help you to internalize the flow of phrases and the imagery utilized.

Again, from my short story, I selected these phrases at random:

One felt as though one were present at the moment of creation when God said: "Let there be light."

It brought the silent, motionless silhouettes to life.

The little groups that had hitherto stood rooted to the earth like desert plants broke into a dance—the rhythm of primitive man dancing at one of his fire festivals at the coming of spring.

Here and there through the smoke, creeping warily under the shadows of tottering walls, emerged occasional men and women.

In addition to lists, your Notebook should serve as your open door to developing the skills of artistic clear communication. Never be satisfied with the first words that come to you in description. Get a copy of Roget's Thesaurus to accompany you in your "Notebook work" and then go out, as did Robert Louis Stevenson, "to note down the features of the scene [before you] or commemorate some halting stanzas." Thus you, as he, will begin to *live* with words!

Again, the challenge of the Notebook is to find "free uninterrupted hours" where you can concentrate on putting words together the best way you can. It is excellent if you can go to a park, sit on the lawn, go inside a beautiful church, wander through an art museum and try to capture the atmosphere, the scenes, the people, the smells, the impressions in words. If you don't have time to take an excursion, sit in your den and try to describe that room in such vivid detail that anyone reading your words would know exactly what the room *looked* like, *smelled* like, *felt* like!

In one of my classes at the college, I brought three girls into the room and asked them to sit before the students who had been assigned to make their first efforts at description in their Notebooks. These are some of the bits I gleaned from my collegians.

She bounces into the room, a long skinny puppet dancing on twisted strings. Big blue eyes, pinocchio nose, and a wide silly smile are pasted on her face. A bitter-sweet mixture of pathos and idiocy, she looks like an elf grown up. . . . The frozen animation begins to melt, and the wooden puppet becomes a real live girl.

The hands, distraught, wrench and tangle themselves together, flying spasmodically to soothe the aching face.

She rocks and jostles her tennis racquet like someone's baby whom she cannot embrace as her own.

She wasn't happy, but I don't know why.

Her blue eyes crinkled at the corners when she smiled.

Straight from high school, infecting a collegiate world with her pleated skirt and plaid blouse-sweater combination.

Conservative girls make very nice wives. You can tell at a glance. In twenty years, she will still look very neat—very clean—very well-pressed. She will still be wearing the plain conventional black shoes and neutral hose, the same wool shirt waist dress, the same plain glasses, and the same trim brown hair.

She sits, sphinx-like.

Her rounded shoulders were now more rounded as if instead of the weight of burdens, she had actually been carrying around twenty pound sacks of cement.

When she sat down, she gazed dreamily toward the heavens almost as if anticipating St. Peter himself to poke his head down through the clouds to share her joy.

When she came in, she was wielding her tennis racquet like David wielding his slingshot before he killed Goliath.

These excerpts came from college students who had never before tried their hands at good description. I hope their efforts will excite you to begin.

An airport, a bus station, a schoolroom, a doctor's office, a church group, waiting lines at checker's counters. Wherever there are people, and you have some idle moments, your Notebook should be in hand striving to "capture" those people in words . . . preserve their idiosyncracies . . . record their uniqueness.

Wherever you go, train your mind to try to capture what is before you in words. Here are some selections from my students' Notebooks of other "word pictures" than "people portraits."

The sky is a delicious color of blue—that color that makes me want to pin a pattern to the heavens and cut myself a dress . . . or a dream.

Sometimes when my body is just walking, my spirit gets so excited it runs on ahead and leaves the rest of me behind!

If they'd make baking apples into perfume, I'd buy it. . . . I love cinnamon, brown sugar, dark apples in dark syrup, and a flaky crust. I hate the greenish-yellow apples under a tan and thin crust.

Did you ever have a memory hit you so hard it actually jerked tears from your eyes? [Note the impact of that strong verb?]

Pomegranate—the outside looked like a badly bruised apple or disfigured acorn squash. The inside was little sacs of pea-like rubies—a bright pink. The little bunches were separated by a thick membrane. The aroma was somewhat like fresh garden peas. Pure freshness.

The clouds looked like they'd been sleeping face down on a chenille bedspread . . . or perhaps like a corrugated tin roof . . . or a crinkled potato chip!

It was startling: the contrast. The blood spilled from a gory battle in the sky. No, that was too sinister. Perhaps it was just that Autumn had dumped a bucket of red paint on that tree. The outside leaves remained green and unaffected, but the middle was definitely red. Yes. Like it or not . . . it was blood red.

To be alone is to pick flowers by yourself . . . to laugh and hear an echo.

How moody the night—heavy, dark, poignant; cold, misty, pressing. On the air a trumpet lingers from the college practice hall. Otherwise all is quiet, still, encompassing. A time to rest, to dream, to be. I think night was a good idea.

These "gleanings" from collegians' Notebooks will give you the challenge I am offering to you. Make time in your schedule to spend with your Notebook deliberately striving to draw the most graphic word pictures of everything you *see, hear, smell, touch, feel.* Your lists, your increasing sensitivity to verbs and phrasing, your Thesaurus, and your practice will begin to transform the way you put words together and you will be on your way to Writing Creatively!

The diary/Journal is for self-exploration with no thought of technique.

The Notebook is for brain-stretching concentrated focus on technique.

In the Journal, you are concerned only with capturing thoughts, ideas, emotions in tangible form.

In the Notebook, you are concerned only with presenting those thoughts, ideas, emotions in the most graphic explicit language possible.

7

THE SENSES

Every person has five senses! That's what I wrote on a third-grade test paper. And although my teacher thought that was the right answer . . . it isn't right at all FOR THE WRITER! Because, you see, YOU ARE A SPECIAL BREED!

Let's consider the senses that a writer has and must ever strive, in the Notebook and Journal, to develop!

1. Sight

A writer *sees* diverse levels, diverse radiances, diverse shadings, diverse reactions. A writer *never* sees a brown tree with green leaves. Look for all the innuendos of grays and yellows blended in. *Strive* to capture all of the stance, personality, and character of the tree in words. A writer *never* sees "another person!" Look at a unique special person with his/her own peculiar background of tears and joys. Sit in an airport and try to capture in words the look, feel, and emotion of *a* personality who sits there bored . . . or reading Dickens . . . or sagging with pain-filled eyes. The third-grade teacher was right: Probably the most important sense is sight! But *you* must *see* more than meets the careless eye!

2. Hearing

A writer *hears* diverse levels, diverse meanings, diverse reactions, diverse emotions. A writer *never* just hears someone talk. Listen for the tonal quality, the rapidity of voice, the emotional nuance. Words don't mean; people do! And you can only catch *meaning* through acutely sensitive ears.

The college freshman *says:* "I hate this college! The food is terrible! The plumbing is stopped up! The professors are boring!" The college freshman *means:* "I'm terrified. I don't know what to do or how to behave in this new world. Hold my hand! Help me!"

It didn't take my husband long, after our marriage, to understand that when I vehemently SAID that nothing was wrong . . . SOMETHING WAS! The third-grade teacher was right: hearing is a basic sense. But YOU must HEAR more than words!

3. Touch

A writer develops every facet of touch. Pull off your shoes and walk barefoot in the snow, on dew-wet grass, on sunbaked sand, on a football field after a game. Rub your cheek on a velvet dress, on your husband's tweed jacket, on a cold windowpane. Consciously focus on the touch of water as you sink into a hot tub, the splat of a snowball in your face, the warmth of flannel cuddling your body.

Hands are certainly one of the most important means of touch. Our hands are extensions of our heart. Through their movements, people know what we are, who we are, and how we feel. We can discover the same by observing and touching their hands. Take hold of someone's hand. Focus and you can feel the beating of their heart, the very substance of their life. The hand has as many reactions as the face. Consider: hands covering the face in desperate moments . . . hands reaching out for warmth . . . hands caressing a baby with love . . . hands clawing to push death away . . . hands tense in holding something tangible or intangible . . . hands clapping in happiness . . . hands knotting in loneliness.

The shape of the hands follows the structure of the body:

heavy, thin, muscular, fragile, strong, smooth, rough. Our mind is the energy. Our hands are the projection of that energy.

The hands are beautifully sensitive to nature. Feel the bark of the tree; put your hands in the snow; run your fingers across the sand; put your hands near a fire; hold your hands up to the rain or the sun or the wind; run your hands over the coat of your dog or the skin of a snake. Each is a different feeling, all its own . . . both tactically and emotionally. Try to capture that feeling in words.

As the years pass, your hands gain knowledge as does your mind. They grow older as does your body. Study the hands of an older person. You can see episodes of their life: scars, stains, callouses, scratches. Write about what you learn about that person through a touch of those hands!

The third-grade teacher was right: touch is a basic sense. But you must develop that tactile sense in every fiber of your being. As you do, you will learn more than mere sensory experiences to share . . . you will learn about LIFE itself.

4. Taste

One of my college students was asked to do an assignment trying to capture *taste* in words. This is her response: "I sat in the dining room and tasted the American chop suey. It was rock-hard granules of meat, slimy elbows of macaroni, lukewarm mushy tomato, thin transparent skin of grease. My stomach rebelled, thinking of the crunchy flaky chicken, snow-mounds of potatoes, and the mountain of chocolate cake with rivulets of icing flowing down its sides that was now reposing on my mother's table at home. I started to get up when a girl sitting by me commented: 'Isn't this delicious?' At my incredulous stare, she confided that her family lived on food stamps and any dish with meat in it was a rarity. I did an immediate taste-bud transformation and ate the food before me with relish."

Note her use of description to make the reader TASTE with her . . . note the insight gained through the sense of taste. So, even on this level, the writer must be more *astute* than the third-grade teacher imagined when she set down taste as a basic sense. It is a powerful tool of description when developed.

5. Smell

What can your nose tell you? Amazing things. Begin to note the aromas about you: perfumes, colognes, different food smells, wood burning, rubber burning, pine trees in the rain, hospital ammonia, the mixture in a doctor's office, the mixture in an airplane, a new baby, a sun-drenched morning. What memories, perceptions, emotions are stirred by smells? Strive to answer that question in detail. Let your mind examine how smell colors our world.

When I think of the smell of chalkboards, I remember first grade and my tense excitement; third grade and my fear that the problem solved by my hand on the board was incorrect; seventh grade when I got out of class early to "clean" the erasers; college where, leaning against a chalkboard in an empty classroom, Bill kissed me the first time. This important sense must be developed for a full photograph of an experience.

The third-grade teacher was right: smell is a basic sense but its connotations are vital to *you*. Try to capture the exact essence of aromas in words for good description, and more; strive to perceive and express the connotations each involves.

6. Sense of the Specific

Now we leave the third-grade teacher behind. Perhaps, of all the senses, this is the most indispensable to the writer. Sight, the most important of the basic five, would not prevent a person from sharing thoughts were it taken away. The sense of the specific must always be operative if a person is to communicate effectively.

The writer *never* deals in generalities. He is forever concerned with detail of A particular item, person, or event. My family has always teased me that they need not bother to go anywhere I go because I can tell them every last detail of color, vocal inflection, facial innuendo, and eye expression. And they assure me of the hundreds of *boring* hours they have spent in their lives listening to *detail!* Detail, which if they were present at the same function, they did not even notice!

This sense of the specific is the one on which the writer must become the most acutely sensitive. I will tell you over and over: DON'T TELL ME; SHOW ME! And you cannot show me except through the use of SPECIFICS!

Get a book written by your favorite author and begin to search through it for his/her sense of the specific. If he/she is really good, you will see it all the way through. You will know that the protagonist did not eat breakfast . . . that is *telling* the reader! Instead your writer will draw a word picture of the table set with yellow tablecloth and pink-rose-scalloped dishes to which the protagonist brings a huge platter centered with slabs of succulent ham surrounded with golden steaming eggs.

It is the specific that draws word pictures. It is the specific that gives insight. When you observe an austere, dignified, serious physician writing out a prescription, you notice the specific detail that he is wearing cuff links that sparkle "I am loved!" Instantly, you know that doctor has a sense of humor, a sense of romanticism . . . you know that he has a life that is important to him beyond professional medicine . . . and he becomes a person for the first time.

7. Sense of the General

Not only does the writer have an acute sense of detail, but you must be able to perceive the overall scope. When one understands the specifics of an idea, a philosophy, a person, or an event, what do they all add up to? What is the general lesson that can be learned? What is the over-arching horizon? What is the inference that can be deducted from the small to the large? This is an imperative.

From the specifics, one builds a general foundation on which one's life's philosophy, actions, and reactions will rest for always. For example, when I first answered the specific question: Is there a God?, I proceeded to ask a second specific question: What is God like? Then I tackled a third: What will be my relationship to God as I live and plan my future? In answer to those three answers of detailed specificity, I could, then, arrive at the all-encompassing foundation on which all events of my life would rest.

Another example: Marie is my friend. She is black. She grew up in the ghetto of Kansas City. Because I know Marie, in the specific, I have a basis on which I may build my sense of the general. I can discuss the black problem with some degree of knowledge in the total scope of society which is an important attribute for the writer. You must be able to see relationships . . . make inferences . . . and generalize so that you can deal with universalities.

8. Sense of History

An advertisement on television for a book detailing World War II entices: "Learn about the war that determined the way your children live!" It's a good gimmick line . . . but it's more. It's true. Think of how different our culture would be had the war not occurred. Think of how different our culture would be had America not won the war.

The writer needs to have a keen knowledge of the past and its implications for the present and future. When first shown on TV, the movies *Roots* and *Holocaust* poignantly spotlighted the need for an understanding of history. One of my childhood chums is Jewish.

After viewing *Holocaust,* she wrote me: "I grew up with music lessons, lollipops, and roller skates just like you. I was not a part of the Holocaust nor did I hear it discussed in my family. But my grandfather was a victim of the madness and the responses of my grandmother, my father, my uncles have colored much of my development. And I was unaware. It was all invisible, insidious, emotional . . . unarticulated . . . but totally pervasive. I never understood myself until I watched the movie. As I understood past horror in my family, I came to understand much more of me."

History books, television documentaries, history courses on educational television are all assists to the writer. The more you know of the past of humanity, the more you can understand the present and forecast the future.

Steve Allen's excellent series on PBS, "Meeting of Minds," presents the great minds, the great personalities, the great human forces in human history. When you can participate in that show, you will learn from whence much philosophy, ideas, culture have emerged. And when you understand the past, you can, more likely, speak with expertise and wisdom about the present and future.

9. Skepticism

Does this surprise you? I'm not asking you to develop cynicism. Far from that! I believe the best writers are constantly filled with wonder and awe. But alongside that excited-child spirit is the intelligent searching mind that *demands* answers! The writer can never accept a cliché! The writer can never accept something as truth just because someone said it was so . . . no matter how beloved or how wise is that person. The writer *has* to learn through the agony of his own emotions . . . he *has* to journey through the footsteps of his own experience. The good writer is always asking and *reasking* good, tough questions. And seeking ever-more-thorough, articulate, *honest* answers.

One of the things I loved most about my father was his skepticism. He was fifty-three years of age when I was born, so if there ever should have been a generation gap between child and parent, it should have been between us! But it wasn't. Because he was so willing to keep an open mind. When I was in high school, I asked permission to do something and horrified, from standards on that subject in his youth, he gave me a resounding NO! The next morning, he told me I could participate. Amazed, I said: "But last night . . ."

He stopped me with a line that still delights me. He said: "Just because I believed that last night does not necessarily mean that I believe it today!"

The writer has a demanding, searching, inquiring mind that is always in gear. When he finds satisfying answers, he firmly implants them and stands on them to tackle bigger questions. But he's never afraid to reask basic questions whenever the need arises. Fluidity, flexibility, growth, willingness to learn and change are all wrapped up in the sense of skepticism, which is vital for the *thinking* writer.

10. Sense of People

The writer always is concerned with a *person*. I remember a tea at the university I attended where I was the honoree for some achievement. I was introduced to a professor who said: "Oh yes, you're in my third-hour class." That was true. I was a part of that lump of faces defined in his mind as "third hour." He was not a writer.

At that same tea, I was introduced to another professor who said: "Oh yes, you attended a seminar of mine yesterday. You wore a red coat that matched your boots perfectly. And you were completely out of breath when you arrived. I assumed you must have run all the way up the hill (KU is on top of Mount Oread and students park at the bottom and, when always late as was I, they run to the top of the mountain, to the top of the building, to the classroom designated). You are very expressive," the lady went on, "because I could play on your face like it was a piano! Ah! And you take notes in shorthand! How clever of you!" *She* was a writer.

To her, I was a *person*. Not a part of a lump called "third hour"!

When my parents married, it was during the time when courtship was strictly supervised and limited. My father was a dynamic young preacher who lived in another state, so he did not see my mother, even under the austere conditions, as often as another beau. My mother was a beautiful young schoolteacher who played the piano. They were married . . . and to their dismay . . . they discovered that dynamic preachers don't marry beautiful schoolteachers! PEOPLE marry PEOPLE! And so they had to get acquainted with each other as individuals from the first "Hello."

The writer can never make that mistake. People, for *you,* can never be "third hour" . . . or preachers . . . or schoolteachers . . . they have to be unique, one-of-a-kind, never-before-on-earth, never-to-be-again *individuals*.

11. Sense of Self

The writer *must be* self-centered. Now before you write me off, note that I did not say "selfish!" I said, "self-centered," which means that you put yourself in the center of the world and look about. "How would I feel if I were in my parents' position now?" "How would I feel if I had to retire from the Army after living it for thirty years?" "How would I feel if I were asked to take in the child of my husband's first marriage when that had not been in the initial agreement?"

With your own emotions, perceptions, and understanding, strive to look out on the world from as many windows as possible. You have to use as your only frame of reference your own emotions, intelligence, and imagination. And to do this effectively, you must *know yourself*. You must *understand yourself*. You must comprehend human limitations and strengths as you find them *in yourself*. It will require a great deal of effort, hard work, honesty, agony, and tears to develop this sense . . . but it is imperative if you would write.

12. Sense of Implication

The writer looks ahead. Having looked back through history, you view the current status, the directions of its changing flux, and wonder what implications all of this has for the future. How are events shaping and determining destiny? The development of this sense enables you to determine the significant from the insignificant . . . and from your vantage point, look toward the future of individuals, groups, society, our world.

An important example would be the need for a writer concerned with marriage and family life to understand the history of that institution in America, its current evolvement to the extremes of free love and communes, and make intelligent, learned implications for its future. This sense is developed chiefly through conscious effort, through deliberate study.

13. Sense of Problems

This probably sounds strange, but I believe it is a vital attribute of the writer. Too many people allow themselves to get trapped in the maze where viability can be lost. The writer needs to search for specific, identifiable problems with*in* the maze. When this occurs, the writer can know how to reach for viable solutions.

Whether writing about personal life or creating a short story, this sense of sorting out problems and thinking through to specific answers is imperative.

14. Sense of Solutions

Although inherent in the discussion above, I felt this should be spotlighted singly. As in developing the sense of implication, this power of solution-finding is developed by deliberate practice and study. Although the writer ultimately wants to arrive at the solution that makes the most sense personally, you can do that more intelligently if you study the solutions that have satisfied other men.

These mind stimulators will help you find a more definitive answer, as a rule, than if you merely sit down for skull cracking on your own. I used to assign my students a problem paper. They chose their own problem—unanswered prayer, high rate of unemployment, injustice—then they were asked to research in depth the answers recorded of other minds' grappling with the problem and, on that foundation, graphically state their personal solution.

A writer must be acutely equipped with the sense of identifying and isolating problems. But that is only the first step. You must ever develop through wide study and mind-stretching thought the *sense of solutions*. In a way, isn't that what writing is all about?

15. Sense of Reading

Eugenia Price once said that if she could arrange her life exactly as she would like, she would do three things: read, write, and eat steak. I think that is probably true of most writers, although personally I would prefer to eat chocolate pie!

One not only must be a *reader* in order to learn factual information that is vital, but a writer must *read* in order to receive mind-stimulating concepts . . . and you must *read* in order to gain a sense of *audience* . . . which simply means that, through reading, you gain ideas, impulses, feelings, philosophies, cultures that are different from yours . . . and you observe how communication between writer/reader can occur . . . even across bar-

riers. Reading is probably your best means of gaining this understanding.

Although I am not an athletic fan, but wanted to share in
family fun, I went to every football and basketball game while we
were at The University of Kansas. But I also carried a book. While
others yelled and acted crazy, I read. I was often introduced by my
husband's friends: "She's the one with the book!"

And that is a fairly apt description of most writers, I think. If
not writing (or eating steak or chocolate pie!), she's "the one with
the book!"

16. Sense of Involvement

The writer is involved in all facets of life. Not a detached
observer . . . but one who is really involved. As a college professor, I used to watch the freshmen trying to enroll . . . and often
I would literally find tears in my eyes as I *felt* the students'
desolate emotions of isolation in the teeming throngs. In high
school, he was student-council president; in high school, she was
Homecoming Queen. But here, each is *lost* in the masses of
other STUCO presidents and dozens of other Homecoming
Queens! And when they came to me for registration counsel, I
would become so *involved* with their personal feelings that it took
hours instead of minutes to get an enrollment card signed.

A writer "is a person with his skin off" . . . always feeling,
caring, trying to understand, sharing, wanting to help. A writer is
always involved! It is a sense that you, as a writer, are born with.
I challenge you to *develop it!*

17. Sense of Detachment

Now . . . let me contradict myself! But it's true! The writer is
more deeply involved than the average person, while a certain part
is totally detached! And it is that part that observes, gains a
comprehensive view of a situation, makes implications, identifies
problems, and begins reaching for solutions.

One of the times I was most aware of this dual set of senses
was immediately following diagnosis in 1974. With returning life,

I whirled up and down hospital hallways, making friends on every floor, chatting and visiting with in-bed patients as though I were still a minister's wife. A detached part of me stood aside and watched this vibrant, in-love-with-life person and remembered her. From the far, dusty past. There had been an exuberant joyful person who was *involved* with everybody who touched her life . . . but she had died. In the slow slide into physical death prior to diagnosis, the spirit of me had already died. I moved only with iron grim will power. Now resurrected, with the body flooded with the life-essential hormones, the detached part of me looked on with great interest at life reborn. The excitable, people-loving part of me was *involved* . . . but the detached part of me observed, recorded, assimilated, and perceived the lessons that were important to learn. I would not place one as more important than the other. I would place great value on both *involvement* and *detachment*.

18. Sense of Curiosity

The writer is forever *astonished* at the obvious, delighted with the usual, determined to know *why* about everything! You need to develop this sense. Our educational system downplays it almost to obliteration. As an adult, you may have to deliberately set about rekindling it. Look for the whys and wherefores not only of ideas . . . but of people . . . and customs . . . and experiences. Explore museums and fire stations, art galleries and police buildings, symphonies and courts of law. Because of my illness, I have discovered the wonders of educational TV (as well as some prime-time shows), which can take a viewer to more parts of the world . . . inside more kinds of organizations and institutions than one could ever do in a lifetime of actual visitation. Curiosity will open up a thousand new worlds to you in a thousand different ways. The writer should never be bored!

19. Sense of Irony

I suppose one may define irony as the most intelligent form of humor and you need to develop it to the highest degree possible. You should be both an idealist and a realist . . . and irony is what makes it possible for you to live with *what ought to be* and *what is!* And with that, you can charm the most reluctant reader.

20. Sense of Form

The writer must develop an instinct for the best pattern into which to put the particular insights for which there is the desire to share: poetry? short story? essay? anecdote? meditation? Your thoughts and concepts must be placed in the proper mold to bring a wholeness, a completeness to your discussion. There is always a *best* form for each particular idea. Widening your knowledge of the forms available and sharpening your skill in using each of them is an imperative.

21. Sense of Words

The writer is in love with words. What is more exciting than being able to select specific words to say specific things in a newly specific way? In all of your reading . . . in all of your listening . . . in all of your study of the Thesaurus and the dictionary . . . build your vocabulary . . . but more . . . build *your* style of putting words together. There is a uniqueness to *you* that will give uniqueness to your expression that will become your trademark and your sheer joy. Love words . . . study them . . . make lists of them . . . toy with them . . . find new ways of using them . . . develop, in the fullest measure possible, your own sense of words, your personal uniquely inimitable STYLE!

Notice the use of many of the writer's *special* senses that are used in the following pieces. Become sensitive to the use of these senses in all of your reading . . . most especially in all of your writing. God gave you the sensory gifts. What you do with them is your gift to Him.

Consider the various senses at work in these pieces.

WINTER IS . . .

Roseanne Bergantine Giencke

The door to winter opens with the first snowflake that drifts down, deceptively innocent, from a gray, blustery sky. And until the last flake falls and is swallowed up by the soil, savagely thirsty after its seasonal slumber, its icy reign is felt across the land.

Winter is nature's beauty and its weather is as the capricious woman whose moods are uncertain and constantly changing. Winter is a time when trees switch green frocks for snow stoles and sun-sparkling glaze is draped about their limbs like diamond bangles. The ground becomes a rumpled sheet of shimmer white; blizzards plow through prairies and snow huddles into drifts in house corners to evade the wind's wrath. Many consider winter their favorite season. Others feel it too fierce and fickle to merit their esteem. Yet they too will admit awareness of its fascinating, if somewhat frigid, allure.

Winter is boot prints in the snow and delicate designs swirled deftly upon windowpanes. It is blue jays reprimanding juncos at a bird feeder and rabbits romping under a winter moon. It is the silky gray beards of eavesdropping icicles and the black velvet of night skies, pierced throughout by stars like so many sequinned hatpins.

Winter is rising early to shovel the driveway before breakfast, and having breakfast in morning darkness. It is digging out quilts from the storeroom, frowning over the monthly heating bills, being jolted into wakefulness on weekends by the roar of snowmobiles rather than lawn mowers. It is looking longingly at travel agency show windows, which, come first snowfall, blossom with posters of the sunny Southland.

Winter is Christmas decorations strung along Main Street and pine-fragrant bonfires whose fiery beauty finger-numbed skaters appreciate fully as well as its light and heat. Winter is making popcorn to munch while reading romance novels and shivering through murder thrillers on dismal afternoons. It is people practicing togetherness to defy the forces of nature. It is hot cocoa with a marshmallow within; it is blurry eyes, ruddy cheeks, frozen toes, mittened hands. . . .

Winter . . . it spells cold frosty weather. Yet there is an undefinable, intangible warmth to it that is the envy even of the summer months.

LORD, ACCEPT MY BELATED THANKS

Ruth Vaughn

I thank You, Lord, that You have not diminished the beauty of the rainbow, the grace of a cottontail, or the luminous loveliness of summer for lack of praise from me. I am grateful, Lord, that You have not withdrawn a note from the haunting music of the wind, the excitement of the cold, wild spray of blowing rain, the enchantment of the breeze and oaks exchanging secrets, because of my negligent gratitude. I thank You, Lord, for not leaving unfinished one golden leaf, one tickling raindrop, one mischievous, slender moonbeam because of my sleeping thankfulness.

I am grateful, Lord, for grumbling thunder which rattles winter stars together, for the lazy coils of morning that unwind slowly into a lovely day, for protesting jays and sequestered thickets, for sprinkles of stars, scatter-pinned on the velvet folds of the heavens, for giddy, gay robins to announce the arrival of spring, for the glory of a young pear tree in bridal veil.

I thank You for the diverse radiances of dawn, the crystal-ringed fishpond, the laughter of little children, the bedstead initialed by small convalescents, the quicksilver moments of love and happiness.

Lord, now I pause in a moment of thanksgiving. I know that it is long overdue. For the beauty with which You have filled my world has been taken for granted by me far too long. Accept my gratitude for Thy salvation, a place to serve, friends who love and care, a challenge for which to work, a hope to hold to my heart, a dream to hang onto the very loveliness of spring.

And, most of all, Lord, thank You for taking time from engineering Your planets, Your moons, Your suns, Your stars to bend above me, listening to my cry for help; and even though I am often ungrateful and always unworthy, You care for me. You love me. You answer my prayer!

Though belated and long overdue, Lord, accept my thanks!

8

THE COMPRESSION

Ralph Waldo Emerson said: "Poetry teaches the enormous force of a few words." Because compression and the choice of the most potent words is so vital for the writer, let's look at the poetic form of Japanese expression called Haiku.

When I was a student, I was informed that the characteristics of Haiku were three:

(1) It was a poem containing seventeen syllables in a *set* arrangement per line: 5, 7, 5. *No variation* is allowed.
(2) It was a poem expressing an emotion associated with a season of the year.
(3) It was a poem depicting a spiritual insight.

In addition to these three characteristics, I was told that because of the conciseness demanded, the poem need not be syntactical. In other words, the poem could be structured of related phrases or interrelated words which composed pictures.

Japan has four distinct seasons and, therefore, it is easier for the Japanese poet to use symbolic words than the American. For example, strong winds indicate winter to the Japanese. I grew up in West Texas and strong winds meant every day of the year. The American poet must, therefore, be more explicit in stating "icy winds" or "balmy winds" which give totally different connotations.

There are some three thousand words indicating seasons in Japanese, but such a list is not available in a country where the four seasons are not so uniform. However, there will be times when you can indicate obliquely the season; for instance, "crickets singing" would indicate the warm season from the cold and no further identification would be necessary. Another example of not stating a season, but giving it, is in one of my favorite Haiku translated by Babette Deutsch.

> The falling flower
> I saw drift back to the branch
> Was a butterfly.

The word "butterfly" tells us it is spring.

Another characteristic of the Haiku is obvious in this example. The "spiritual" or emotional response is initiated in the implied loveliness of a flower falling gracefully to earth. It is enlarged when one realizes that the inference had been too quick for the "flower" is "falling" *to* the branch rather than *from* it. The Japanese call this "poetic shock."

Note that in the "spiritual" or emotional aspect of the Haiku, it is merely drawing a word picture. To use my favorite phrase, it is *showing;* never telling. It is about what *is* and nothing more. No commentary of the poet is allowed.

Haiku uses only specifics; never generalities. Simile, metaphor, and other descriptive devices so common in the English language are not available for the writer of Haiku. This is the poetry of what is here and now. It is composed of strong nouns and verbs. There are few modifiers.

When I first began work with Haiku, I spent a great deal of time counting syllables on my fingers. I was more concerned with this arithmetic than any other part of the writing . . . because my professor was! Although I believe this was excellent discipline for the beginning writer, it did turn the focus on the less important. Professor Kamatero Yagi, of Matsuyama University, has written that seventeen English language syllables translate into as many as twenty to twenty-four *jion* (symbol/sounds in Japanese). So although many still feel a Haiku is not a Haiku unless the syllable count is *exactly* 5, 7, 5, Professor Yagi indicates that the more pertinent definition of Haiku would be a poem that meets the last two characteristics in a line-count syllable-structure that is short/long/short. Although the 5, 7, 5 is still the goal for which to strive, it is not essential.

Of greater concern is the line ending . . . for each line must contain a complete thought. Only in rare instances should there be a run-on line in a poem you want to call Haiku.

Although the three lines should be complete thoughts within a whole, it is not made up of three sentences.

Note:

> First crop of green grain
> Goggle-eyed crickets background
> Thanksgiving anthems.

> Robots in routine
> Pause to watch a butterfly
> Hearts become human.

Haiku is an instant of extraordinary awareness . . . when the poet observes a commonplace sight with new perception. A noted student of Zen, Alan Watts, has called this perception the "thusness of things." Haiku is seasonal expression portraying the "thusness of things." According to Japanese philosophy, Man/Nature/Haiku are all part of the same Whole.

Haiku is the highest "tightrope" for the writer for it challenges you, in the most succinct form possible, to *show* and never *tell!* Although a form of simplicity, Alan Watts calls it "the most sophisticated of all poetic forms." It is not just a small poem. It is a word picture of the "thusness of things" . . . the distilled essence of a humanly universal experience with the world of nature.

Its beauty will be joy for you. Its discipline will be of extraordinary benefit in your goal of expression. Probably more than any other art form, it demands that you SHOW ME! Not TELL ME!

Study books of Haiku. They are prolific in your local bookstore or library. Many of these will be translations, so the syllable count or even line count will not be true. But aside from that technicality lost in translation, you will enjoy the word pictures. And their examples will inspire you to develop your own senses necessary for such description . . . and its "tightrope" form will discipline your verboseness. Through writing Haiku, you can have the best training in the art of compression.

Start a Notebook in which you only write Haiku. After you get into it, you may want to start several Notebooks . . . where you write Haiku dealing with diverse subjects.

When we first moved to Colorado, I was so enchanted with the grandeur of the Rockies that I would take an entire afternoon and drive through them, stopping at scenic points to write Haiku description of my emotional response to such beauty. That entire notebook is filled with three-line vignettes of the personal "feel" of Colorado for me.

When I was completing my master's degree, it was late summer. Because of the intensity of the pressure to polish the thesis, prepare for examinations, conclude an entire degree, every fiber of my being was especially sensitive.

Every reaction was extreme.

I could dash past a long-familiar tree on the peak of Mount Oread and find tears of wonder streaming down my cheeks.

Details were clear-cut.

Beauty was highlighted.

Gratitude to God for this academic world where I had experienced such challenge, such achievement overwhelmed!

It occurred to me that a book of Haiku could be my best means of preserving the rioting emotions, could be my best gift to God, Who had allowed me to experience all this joy.

That book today is one of my most prized possessions.

In those three-line expressions, I find a succinct, kaleidoscopic, full-orbed record of the "thusness of things" of my excitement, of my thanksgiving, of my worship in that specific life season.

Books of Haiku are inimitably beautiful ways of sharing. Not only in recordings of your experiences as I have mentioned, but also in expressing gratitude to a friend, making promises to a lover, writing praise to your God.

One, or several Haiku, make personally meaningful "greeting cards" for special days, for special people on any day!

One of my friends, an expert in needlepoint, often writes a Haiku on canvas in fancy lettering. She, then, needlepoints the poetry . . . decorating it with other bits of needlepoint. Her home and the homes of many of her friends and family are brightened and personalized because of her creative sharing. She wrote the Haiku for a special reason, for a special person, and then preserved it in the beauty of needlepoint.

I, who am a cake-decorating "nut," have even written personal Haiku on important cakes for people I love. One of my students embroiders Haiku on pillowcases.

Because of its special qualities, there is *no limit* to the *usefulness* of Haiku in self-expression, God-worship, sharing with others. *And* in all that fun, you are practicing the discipline necessary for every writer to learn: compression. Saying "much in little" is good writing. Perhaps the best way to develop that skill is through prolific use of Haiku.

Don't you love this one?

> Evening star wishes
> Never to come true and yet
> Butterflies on wing.

9

THE RULES

Young writers are too hasty. They are usually entirely satisfied with their first efforts and this viewpoint is fatal to success . . . I find that the majority of young writers won't take advice after it is freely given.

—*Mary Roberts Rinehart*

At the age of eleven, T. N. Alexakos wrote a novel and was "hooked" on the art of writing forever. Of his experience, he said:

It took a few years and stacks of scribbled pages before I realized there was more to putting one word after another than just saying it as you feel or think. I was learning about rules and finding there's a great difference in not writing according to the rules when you don't know the rules and not writing according to the rules when you know them. . . . Those who wish to write and be serious about it must know the language and it's a never-ending discipline.

One of the most difficult things to impress upon the beginning writer is the imperative of *not* being satisfied with "first efforts" . . . but being willing to learn the rules of effectively "putting one word after another" and internalizing those basics so well that they are broken only for some unusual (and deliberate) effect.

If you wanted to become a pianist, you know you would do many finger exercises, scales, arpeggios, and chords before you ever attempted "Rustic Dance" to say nothing of "Beethoven's Fifth."

So with writing.

Consider most of your early efforts as finger exercises . . . writing to build the basic foundation for "Beethoven's Fifth" . . . writing in self-exploration . . . writing to train your brain to think rapidly through your fingers . . . writing to make the rules of "putting one word after another" so much a part of your *inner self* that you can ultimately use them without thought.

I challenge you to make your Notebook a means of becoming so facile in the skill of effective word pictures that you can become the best writer *you* can be! Here are the basics that will help.

Rule 1: Choose the exact word.

> . . . I was reading everything I could put my hands on about bull fighting and one quiet afternoon I realized the bull was always called the "brave bull" and never the "courageous bull." It was my first insight into the [fact] . . . that the dictionary was not . . . the final arbiter as to the meaning of words. Calling a bull courageous would instantly alert every afficianado that you knew little of the business of bulls . . . So it is with writing. [The writer must know] the subtle distinctions in common words.
>
> —T. N. Alexakos

The English language has numerous words for one object in most cases. Only rarely is there *one* word to symbolize something. An example would be the word "lemming" which is the only name we have for that little mouselike rodent. "Purine" is the only word used for a compound whose chemical formula is $C_5H_4N_4$. But for most things, we have words in profusion, all of whose primary meaning is the same but whose connotative meaning will have varying colors. Alexakos points this out when he discusses the fact that brutality and cruelty are, according to dictionary definition, synonymous. And yet there is definitely a difference in meaning. He says: "In a slaughterhouse, there is usually little cruelty although much brutality. At a cocktail party there is seldom any brutality, although you may find a shocking amount of cruelty."

In working with this rule, your Thesaurus will be your best friend. It is so easy to write, using your limited vocabulary, and hoping it is expressive enough. Rarely will it be . . . for your Notebook efforts . . . where you are striving for the most artistic, articulate communication possible.

So take the time to look up the meaning you have in mind . . . peruse the smorgasbord of words in your Thesaurus . . . and *choose* deliberately the word from our language, whose subtle shade of meaning, is *exactly* what you had in mind. Never settle for just the "primary" right word.

Note the different words the Thesaurus lists for the common word Happy.

Beatific . . . Blissful . . . Blithe . . . Cheerful . . . Content . . . Delighted . . . Ecstatic . . . Enchanted . . . Enraptured . . . Exalted . . . Gay . . . Glad . . . Joyful . . . Joyous . . . Overjoyed . . . Rapturous . . . Ravished . . . Rhapsodic . . . Thrilled . . . Elated . . . Cheery . . . Gleeful . . . Jubilant . . . Triumphant . . . Elysian . . . Felicific . . . Winsome . . . and many more.

All of those have the primary meaning we associate with happiness. But there are shades of meaning that give clarity to your expression that is vital. For example, "Rhapsodic" is a word that I should use in trying to "portrait" many of my teenage experiences. A creature of extremes, I literally became "rhapsodic" when joy was mine and my parents would faithfully sit while I gave them every detail of color, nuance, and movement of an event, using the most "rhapsodic" language my sixteen-year-old mind could manage.

Now, at age forty-two, I doubt I shall ever be "rhapsodic" again. God has been good in helping me to "level" out that creature of extremes. Because all the "rhapsodic" highs were terrific . . . the pendulum swung so widely that the depressing lows were excruciating. So now, although happiness comes to me, I doubt "rhapsodic" would ever be the best description of my state again.

Note the word "content" which means happiness to me now, in

an illness that will be with me for life. When I was sixteen, I would have sneered at the word. I wasn't interested in being "content." . . . I wanted to be "thrilled," "enraptured," "triumphant!"

So the first rule you must attempt to internalize is that you never settle for the first word that pops in your mind. Don't be satisfied with primary meanings. Use that Thesaurus to find the word with the *exact* shade of meaning that you want to convey.

Rule 2: Select the specific word. Discard the general.

A general word refers to a group, a class, and a specific word refers to a member of that class. Tree is a general word, but oak, elm, poplar are specific. We must remember, however, that the terms "general" and "specific" are relative, not absolute. Coat, for example, is more specific than garment, for a coat is a kind of garment. But coat, on the other hand, is more general than hunting jacket, for a hunting jacket is a kind of coat. So with our trees above. Oak is more specific than tree but more general than black oak or water oak or post oak. The specific word tends to give color and tang, tends to appeal to the imagination.

—Brockmiler

This rule cannot be overstressed.

The one phrase I wrote more than any other on students' manuscripts in my college classes was this: SHOW ME! DON'T TELL ME! The beginning writer generally falls into the trap to *tell* what happened. The reader doesn't want to be *told;* the reader wants to see . . . hear . . . touch . . . smell . . . feel . . . *be a part of* the experience with the writer.

Don't *tell* your reader that Jill is joyful. *Show* her dancing into her house, throwing wide her arms, and singing: "I could have danced all night!" Your reader sees, hears, feels, and knows, for himself, the truth that Jill is filled with happiness.

Eugenia Price is one of my favorite writers. Here is an example of her use of this rule, which is taken from her book, *The Burden Is Light* (used by permission of the author).

I sat on the patio outside Mother's kitchen door on the top of
the hill and drank black, iced coffee because of the diet and
and smoked and tried not to think. I tried just to look at the
height and depth and green of the top of the grove of ancient
oak trees beneath which our home is nestled just before the
grove moves down over a steep wooded ravine.

I was home again. As all the other years. It was summer.
I liked myself sun-tanned and so set about getting a tan. Dad
brought me sun-tan lotion and a couple of cartons of Camels
the first night and we talked lots of baseball. I knew everyone's major league batting average then. Some of my inner-
unhappiness could have been caused by the Chicago Cubs
and was. But emptiness was more to the point. Dad brought
me sun-tan lotion and Camels and that week's issue of *Variety*
as he always did, and Mother asked me please to lose lots of
weight and showed me her new bird books and we decided
the names of the birds that flocked in bright, quarreling
dozens to the stone bench outside the windows where we ate
breakfast. No one said anything more except how much fun
it was to be home. And how glad we were that Charleston
had its own Class-A baseball club that year.

Note how you, the reader, feel that you are *there*. *You* sit on
the patio . . . not just outdoors. You see the kitchen through the
door rather than simply being on a patio "somewhere." You don't
sip on a drink . . . you don't even sip coffee . . . it is black and
iced! So you not only taste coffee . . . you taste unsweetened
coffee . . . and your teeth get cold instead of hot!

Note that her dad did not bring her cigarettes; he brought
CAMELS. He did not bring her magazines; he brought *Variety*.
Her mother didn't show her a new book. She showed her bird
books and they discussed birds, and you hear them doing it as you
see the birds "flocking" about.

Here, you are invited to participate in the experience the writer
is describing. She doesn't *tell* you that she went home and talked
to her parents who were kind to her. She *shows* you!

Another excellent example of Eugenia Price's expertise in
showing, not telling, is where, in the same book, she relates her

selecting an apartment for herself and her friend who had led her
to Christ. She could have told us that she was unwise in her choice
of a basement room and gone on with the story. But because she
wanted her readers to *share in it with her,* she *showed* us the scene
in these words:

(She has just looked at the ridiculous room) and immediately
[I] leaped wildly and innocently to a completely wrong
spiritual conclusion.
"This," I breathed to myself (remembering Thomas Kelly's
thought about the Inward Light in which everything appears
in an entirely new relationship), "is no doubt God's idea for
me! I've been so high and mighty all my life, most likely He
wants me to learn to live in peasant surroundings like this!"
I feel positive God never wills for any of His children to go
head over heels in debt for something which is sheer madness
in the first place. But following my wrong "guidance" all the
way, with childlike abandon of the few practical maturities I
had inadvertently gathered through the years, I made a profound statement about the Lord taking care of His Own, mis-
quoted the Scripture about Seek ye first the Kingdom and
signed the lease with a flourish almost "comparable" to the
owner's own.
With that flourish, I sentenced Ellen and myself to one year
in a literal dungeon. There was one pipe paneled, pipe ceil-
inged room about ten by fifteen, of dark pocket book brown
with green and yellow candelabra (with flames) painted on
one wall and a purple rooster on the other. Also around the
crooked doorway which led to the adjoining bathroom were
painted green ivy vines. Along one end, just following the re-
frigerator which one always bumped upon entering, ran the
sink and stove or "the lovely modern kitchenette," as the
owner called it with a half-sweep of one hand a full sweep of
the other. At one end of the things that made up the kitchen
was one window which did not open at all. It was sealed shut.
"For your protection," she said, completely discounting air.

Don't you see the writer in her attempts to be deeply spiritual
while doing something totally mad? Don't you see the room and
laugh at the absurdity of the owner's sales pitch? Eugenia Price

did not *tell* you about how she and Ellen came to spend the first year of her Christian life in that room. She *shows* you and you experience it with her and never quite forget it!

ALWAYS PREFER THE SPECIFIC WORD TO THE GENERAL!

ALWAYS SHOW; NEVER TELL!

Rule 3: Use words that express the impression made upon your senses.

> Do not depend on one sense exclusively. . . . If we say "The apple is red," we are not giving a very good impression of the apple. The apple is not only red; it is slick-looking and juicy-looking and fragrant. Our response to the apple is more massive than the response to one sense alone.
>
> —Personal Class Notes

We have already talked about how important a writer's senses are in good expression. This rule points out the added dimension of that imperative in seeking out words that specifically appeal to the reader's senses.

From a College English textbook, I copied this list in my Notebook of Sensory Words. It is mind-stimulating to confront the words that are available in our language that are specifically designed for sensory description. Many of them are not an ordinary part of our vocabulary because we tend to "drift along" with the common ones heard everyday.

Study this list; add to it from your reading, listening, and perusal of the dictionary and the Thesaurus. In your writing, strive to use words that make your reader *feel* with his five senses what you are trying to impart.

Here is the list I began with.

SENSORY WORDS:

TOUCH   chill, clammy, cold, corrugated, grainy, gritty, harsh, jarring, knobby, moist, nubby, numb, plushy, rough, satiny, slimy, slithering, smooth, sting, tingle, tickly, velvety.

TASTE   bland, biting, bitter, brackish, briny, metallic, minty, nutty, peppery, salty, sour, spicy, sweet, tainted, vinegary, yeasty.

SMELL   acrid, fetid, greasy, moldy, musky, musty, pungent, putrid, rancid, rank, reek, stench, sulphurous, woodsy.

SOUND   bellow, blare, buzz, chatter, chime, clang, clatter, cling, crackle, crash, creak, gurgle, hiss, hum, murmur, pop, purr, rattle, rustle, screech, snap, splash, squeak, swish, tinkle, whine, whisper.

SIGHT   blaze, bleary, bloody, burnished, chalky, dappled, ebony, flame, flash, flicker, florid, foggy, gaudy, glare, glitter, glossy, glow, golden, grimy, haze, inky, leaden, lurid, muddy, roiled, sallow, shadow, smudged, spark, streak, tawny, turbid.

I made an assignment for my students to work in their Notebooks on each of these rules. I challenge you to do so.

On the development of sensory expression, specifically, it would be good exercise for you to write sentences which show how each of the above . . . and all the words you add to the list . . . actually work in a sentence to make it good description.

Here is a sample taken from one of my student's first efforts.

SOUND:

1. The giant Kodiak BELLOWED his rage as the heavy slug smashed into his chest.
2. Over the stereo's BLARE, I heard her call my name.
3. I listened to the BUZZ of the crowd. I wasn't a part of it and my heart ached.
4. Her happy CHATTER fills my days with youthful music.
5. The CHIME of my mother's voice in early morning is one of my best memories.

One reason it is so important for you to actually take the time to write out sentences or paragraphs utilizing the rules set forth is that, in such labor, you internalize the new words, the meaning of the rule, and the flow of the language.

The words listed in the English textbook above were, in the

main, limited to one sense. But as was cited in the quote at the beginning discussion of this rule, it is *best* communication when you can find a word that will appeal to more than one sense at a time.

So I suggest that you also begin a list of what my college professor called "polysymbolic" words that appeal to more than one sense. The list he gave us to begin such study with is this one.

WORD	SENSE
Black	Sight
Pitchy	Sight and Touch
White	Sight
Snow	Sight and Temperature
Gray	Sight
Leaden	Sight and Weight
Sticky	Touch
Mucilagenous	Touch and Sight
Sore	Touch
Raw	Touch and Sight
Hot	Temperature
Fiery	Temperature and Sight
Soft	Touch
Cottony	Touch and Sight
Weep	Sight
Sob	Sight, Sound, Motion
Cut	Sight
Chop	Sight, Sound, Motion

Be on the alert to add to this list.

The more fully you can involve your reader in sensory experience, the better will be your communication. Such expertise does not come by thinking "That's nice!" It comes with diligent study of the language and taking the time and effort to make the most comprehensive words a working part of your vocabulary.

In a graduate class, we were once assigned to copy a short story, written by a master, in long hand. My professor's rationale was that, in the task, there was a gaining of melody of language and a perception of the mechanical rules in action that could come no other way. Reading is too quick. Even typing can be too quick.

But actually writing out, word for word, in long hand the way a master-writer puts words together is very helpful.

Although we groaned at the assignment, I agree that it was beneficial. And he assured us that we were indeed fortunate. When he had taken such a class, he had been assigned to copy an entire novel!

In all of your writing in your Notebook, I urge you to take the time to think out or look up in your Thesaurus the *exact* word and the *specific* word rather than the general. But trying to incorporate the newness of sensory words in your vocabulary may take the "finger exercise" of literally writing out sentences using the words you find . . . imbedding them in your language so they will be available to your mind when you need them.

All of the rules, of course, dovetail together.

But you can clearly see how sensory words fit into the imperative of good writing: *Show me! Don't tell me!* If your reader can participate in the experience with his five senses, then it becomes a part of his own life venture. He hasn't read a bunch of words. He has had an event in his own life where he participated sensorially. *That* is significant; *That* the reader remembers; *That* is good writing!

Rule 4: Use active verbs. Strive to avoid the passive tense.

The passive tense always *tells* of mere existence. There are no word pictures in the verb "to be." Try to delete it from your vocabulary completely when an active verb can be used to effect.

Notice the power difference in these examples taken from exercises of this rule in my students' Notebooks:

1. Here is a flower . . . passive.
    Active forms:
    Here wilts a flower.
    Here bounces a flower.
    Here glows a flower.

2. There is a wall.
    There soars a wall.
    There towers a wall.
    There hovers a wall.

3. There is a meadow.
    There sprawls a meadow.
    There stretches a meadow.
    There rests a meadow.

4. Here is the ocean.
    Here tosses the ocean.
    Here roars the ocean.
    Here whispers the ocean.

The strongest form of speech is the verb. Just as I suggested in the beginning discussion of the Notebook, listing powerful verbs and making them a vital part of your vocabulary is *essential*. Use them instead of the passive tense as a general rule.

Note in my students' examples the difference the verb made. Not only does it change the statement from one of mere existence, it gives a sensory image to the statement with no addition of words. Some think adjectives are the best form of description. Not true. Strong verbs can speak concisely and in most instances better than adjectives.

Again, I encourage you to take your Thesaurus and dictionary and write ways of changing the verb "to be" in as many sentences as you can imagine. The varied, the totally diverse, the completely changed picture that emerges because of verb change will increase your sensitivity to this powerful tool in communication.

Note the difference in our impression of the flower in the first example. From the mere statement of the existence of a flower, we have the option of seeing a drooping flower, a flower that is (to use an oft-repeated phrase of Felix Unger in the TV show "The Odd Couple") "cheerful and peppy and bursting with love!" and a flower that makes one's inner spirit warm with beauty.

Change *one* word . . . and the picture, the mood, the message is different.

There's a song about "What a Difference a Day Makes!"

There should be one for writers called "What a Difference *a Verb* Makes!"

Work to incorporate this rule in *all* of your writing.

Rule 5: Make new words from old ones.

To add freshness and originality to your writing, work to combine the old into new arrangements. I found an advertisement in an old *Reader's Digest* entitled "Who's the Blind-spotted Buckwatcher in your house?" (He was the one looking for bargains that were not as good as the one offered in the ad!) But what I want you to notice is the spice in the ad because of the two "new words" "Blind-spotted" and "Buckwatcher." The adman could have talked about the guy who wears blinders in his efforts to watch his dollars, but this is not nearly so catchy as a "Blind-spotted Buckwatcher!"

Here are some examples from my students' Notebooks, which will help you start a list of your own.

Wasp-head; Pin-head; Needle Noggin   (All meaning "Dumb!")
Foot-licker   (A blarney-dealer out for favors)
Snow-dealer   (A student who gave "apples" to professors!)
Door-opener   (Used in a sentence describing their creative writing teacher; I liked that . . . because they were, of course, talking about life's doors!)
Honey-walker   (A particular girl on campus who knew she had a nice figure and showed it)

The use of this rule in their Notebooks is so collegiate that I think it will help you to see that the power of this word formation comes not only in its originality, but from the immediacy, the intimacy it gives in its context. You almost have to have an explanation to understand, but when you do, it's great communication!

Whenever you traditionally are snagged with a simile like "It's hard as a rock!", change it to the more original: "It's rock-hard!" "There were clouds in the sky" is stronger when phrased: "The sky was cloud-studded."

This rule will also take effort on your part. You will have to restructure your ordinary language so that compound words add originality and sparkle to your writing, but it is worth the effort.

Try it! You'll *like* it!

Rule 6: Delete cliché words.

This is hard.

We are so used to using pet words in our vocabulary that we are unaware how often we use them and that such overuse renders them meaningless. Some of the worst offenders are words such as great, nice, wonderful, et cetera. These words have been used so often to mean so many different things that they have no meaning. You can say a girl is great, nice, and wonderful. You can also say a zoo is great, nice, and wonderful. A class is great, nice, and wonderful . . . and you know nothing really about any of the three except it must be pleasant in some way.

I am an expert in discussion of this rule because I fall victim to it so easily. When I wrote my second book: *It's Fun to Be a Girl!*, the editor went through the manuscript and counted the number of times I used the word "wonderful"!

He thought it was funny (albeit a bit unprofessional) . . . but I was appalled!

I had *no* idea I was using such a limited vocabulary!

The reason for that overworked word in that manuscript was that "wonderful" so aptly described my outlook on femininity and the growth into girls' dreams-come-true! But that reason made no difference in the quality of my communication. I had over-used a word until it was meaningless in the manuscript.

I still use the word on occasion because there *are* times I am filled with wonder . . . and it just seems the *best* word! But I try to use it rarely and only when it truly *is* the *exact* word for that moment.

Probably the greatest offender is "very." Writers seem to feel they can add impetus to a statement if they include that adverb. Not so. And because it is superfluous, it weakens the statement. So try to delete it entirely. Only for special effect should you allow that word in usage.

If you will become sensitive to your own language, you will find others. Keep a list of these offenders and try to replace them with diversity of the *exact* words that will have more meaning than the ones that have become cliché.

Rule 7: Delete apologies.

Believe in your own observations, philosophies, and statements. Have the courage to be personally assertive. Terms like:
"It seemed to me" . . .
"If I may say so" . . .
"If I may use the term" . . .
"If I may be so bold" . . . should be cast-offs.
You are the writer.
You are presenting life as you see it.
So state it in declarative sentences without apology. YES . . . you may say so! You may use the term! You may be so bold! You are the writer! You are presenting your subjective account of life. Believe in yourself. Use active, flatly stated verbs. This is your clearest communication of your impressions, philosophies, word pictures.

Rule 8: Perceive likenesses in things diverse.

This is such an important rule . . . but one difficult to come by! It is so easy to say "old tower." The words fit. But why not take an adjective usually given to "old people" or "tired people" and call it an "aching tower"? It gives a totally different impression and a new vitality. . . . doesn't it?

I challenged my students to use this rule in describing a blue sky. Here are some of their efforts:

Master-designed canopy of turquoise
Cotton-candy topping dipped in blue dye
Boy-baby blanket
Deep purple velvet

Some of their efforts to take an adjective generally ascribed to one subject and place it in description of a totally different topic are these:

Cocoa-bark
She expelled acceptance
His eyes slithered over her
Squawking barn
Baby-skinned sunrise

Baby-spanked pink
Lemon-squeezed carpet
Robin-egg dress
Newly hatched woman
Cinnamon-colored ground
Inky hawk
His glance stung her painfully
The path wriggled in the sunlight
He limped on turtle-crutched joints.

Whenever you can combine the vocabularies of two diverse entities, you will create a novel and impressive bit of description.
Some assert that this rule demands a "mystical quality" that comes
only from pure genius. I think that limitation is accepted because
so few writers, other than the great, take the necessary time and
effort to search out the likenesses in things diverse.

I challenge you to become one of those few who do excel!
Don't let this viable tool for description elude you.

Rule 9: Become expert in the use of imagery.

Imagery may be defined as "mental images produced by memory
or imagination." Another definition commonly used is "descriptions and figures of speech." Note the lavish imagery in this familiar Psalm.

The Lord is my shepherd; I shall not want.
He maketh me to lie down in green pastures; he leadeth me
beside the still waters.
He restoreth my soul: he leadeth me in the paths of righteousness for his name's sake.
Yea, though I walk through the valley of the shadow of death,
I will fear no evil: for thou art with me: thy rod and thy
staff they comfort me.
Thou preparest a table before me in the presence of mine
enemies: thou anointest my head with oil; my cup runneth
over.
Surely goodness and mercy shall follow me all the days of
my life; and I will dwell in the house of the Lord forever.

—Psalm 23

This chapter you probably memorized as a child is an ongoing series of vignettes leaping from one to another, vivifying each in a strong floodlight of imagination.

Imagery, in its highest form, relies a lot on rule 8. The imagination is not bound to commonplace expression but transforms the expression into something different, and yet similar. Anne Morrow Lindbergh is an artist of imagery. In her discussion of finding the viabilities of human experience, she wrote: "Even small and casual things take on significance if they are washed in space, *like a few autumn grasses in one corner of an oriental painting,* the rest of the page bare." (Italics mine.)

Not only is rule 8 an imperative in building images, so is rule 3 which deals with sensory words. One of my professors said that "an appeal to the senses is the only way to create images." He went on to assert that "mere factual knowledge is worse than nothing so far as art is concerned. Scientific details are not imaginative. They have no place in artistic writing."

Some of the excellent examples of imagery he gave were: From the Bible: "A living dog is better than a dead lion." (Simply: It is better to have life than death.)

"He that soweth iniquity shall reap vanity." (Simply: Wickedness is vain).

From *Hamlet:*
To be or not to be; that is the question;
Whether 'tis nobler in the mind to suffer
The slings and arrows of outrageous fortune,
Or to take arms against a sea of troubles,
And by opposing end them. (Simply: Is life better than death?)
The morn in russet mantle clad
Walks o'er the dew of yon high eastern hill. (Simply: it is dawn.)

Eugene Field did not merely write that poignant reminders of a dead loved one bring pathos and loneliness, he brought the experience *to* the reader with the imagery of

> The little toy dog is covered with dust,
> But sturdy and staunch he stands;
> And the little toy soldier is red with rust,

And his musket moulds in his hands
. . .
And they wonder, as waiting these long years through,
In the dust of that little chair,
What has become of our Little Boy Blue
Since he kissed them and put them there.

Washington Irving proved himself a master of imagery when he took the concept that it grew darker in Westminster Abbey and phrased it thus: "The chapels and aisles grew darker and darker. The effigies of the kings faded into shadows; the marble figures of the monuments assumed strange shapes in the uncertain light; the evening breeze crept through the aisles into the cold breath of the grave."

The *imagery* makes you experience with the writer. You are no longer reading words. Sensorily, you participate. *That* is good writing.

In your Notebook work, constantly strive to develop the skillful use of imagery. It will make the difference between ordinary and vital communication.

Rule 10: Play the game of "What If?"

This rule will help in developing rule 8; it will assist in stretching your imagination you will want to use in fiction; it will aid in the discovery of wider horizons within yourself and within your world of language. Very simply, it involves taking Notebook in hand and letting your mind run free with the words: "What if . . ." and then suddenly your creative mind will come up with an idea . . . explore it for its content . . . for its audacity . . . its freshness . . . and the new ways it can help you structure your language.

One of my student's work with this rule is given below as stimulus for your efforts.

What if . . . Douglas MacArthur suddenly sat beside me on a cliff overlooking a sea? I'd probably snap to attention like a cadet and be terrified to speak in his authoritarian presence. I'm sure his voice would sound like a cannon and his mind would be bayonet-sharp. And I would crouch at his side like an incoming prisoner handcuffed to his mechanical soldiers.

What if . . . he weren't like that at all? What if his voice lilted like a melody? What if there were laughter doing a tango in his eyes? What if his smile were wistful . . . softening the military face into a waif-like orphan? Then I'd turn to him with happiness, charmed by the unexpected music of a unique self.

Do you see the possibilities in this rule?

Immediately the writer begins "perceiving similarities in things different" . . . probably never had she thought of a "bayonet-sharp mind" or a "cannon voice" until she considered this improbable situation. So the game is a definite friend to rule 8. But more . . . do you see how she could take those two paragraphs and write a story?

Ultimately she did and it was the first thing she ever had published. It all began here in her first working rule 10. His name wasn't Douglas MacArthur in the story, but he was an officer who she approached with trepidation . . . and discovered the man in the second paragraph who ultimately ended the story with a most romantic proposal.

Another student wrote:

What if . . . Mrs. Vaughn lost her voice and hands?

She proceeded into pages of description of the way I would communicate with my toes. It is hilarious as she uses original language that could come only through such an abnormal situation.

This is a rule that can be worked even without pen in hand. I often do it lying in bed . . . just for fun . . . but in the fun, it is stretching the lines of imagination, giving fresh concepts of the way words can be put together, adding originality to my efforts at communication.

It's a good rule. I recommend it.

10

THE FIGURES OF SPEECH

The best writer is the one skilled in the use of "figurative language." Implicitly, "figures of speech" have been a part of most of the basic rules of putting words together effectively. Now it is time to explicitly examine these important tools.

In working with "figures of speech," your Notebook will, again, be your best friend as you make lists, write descriptive sentences, paragraphs, essays, and try to imbed these dynamic tools in the very fiber of your communication. They will help you find the *real* you!

1. Metaphor and Simile.

The greatest thing by far is to be a master of metaphor. It is the one thing that cannot be learned from others; and it is also a sign of genius.

—Aristotle

Very simply a metaphor or a simile may be defined as a comparison. The difference between them is that a simile makes the comparison directly, as a declarative statement. The simile is a stated comparison; the metaphor is an implied comparison.

EXAMPLE:
SIMILE: She was as depressed as a wilted flower.

METAPHOR: Her depression made her a wilted flower.

One of my favorite similes comes from a beloved poem by Amy Lowell in which she tells of a letter coming to tell of her lover's death. She was in the garden and said:

> As I read it in the white, morning sunlight
> The letters squirmed like snakes.

From: *Patterns*

It would seem the simile is stronger in this example than were it stated as a metaphor: "The letters squirmed." That leaves out the image of repulsive snakes.

However I think the metaphor is stronger when you state that the "ship *plowed* through the ocean" than were it stated as a simile, "The ship moved like a plow through the ocean." So each has its own strengths, and selection of simile or metaphor must be made on the individual context.

The major problem with the use of metaphor and simile is that they are such a common part of our language it is easy for us to use the cliché. George Orwell wrote the following observation:

> [Modern writing] consists less and less of words chosen for the sake of their meaning, and more and more of phrases tacked together like the sections of a pre-fabricated henhouse. . . . There is a huge dump of worn-out metaphors which have lost all evocative power and are merely used because they save people the trouble of inventing phrases for themselves. . . . Modern writing at its worst . . . consists in gumming together long strips of words which have already been set in order by someone else.

So, as you begin striving to develop the facility of simile and metaphor (which Aristotle believed is the greatest mastery of all writing skills), do heed Orwell's well-founded comment.

Don't be willing to settle for the well-worn comparisons of our language. You know the ones: "I'm as cold as ice!" "She wallowed in self-pity!" "He's hard as nails!"

Those are such oft-said phrases that all sparkle is gone from them. Make your similes and metaphors as spontaneously original as *hard work* can manage!!

GROWTH

Southern pines pierce the sky,
Fearless in aspiring height and dignity,
In verdant growth.
And were you not aware, at sapping time,
Nor did not recognize scar-tissue
In a pine,
You would never even guess the wounding,
Incisive, draining, deep.

Sometimes, a man lets God regard him
As the pines.
Then we, with faltering tongue and
Heart,
Strive for an apt description.
But God does not.
Comes His promise,
Comes His presence,
"Holy."

—Sallie Chesham,
from *Walking with the
Wind,* copyright © 1969,
p. 47; used by permission
of Word Books, Publisher,
Waco, Texas 76703

Underline the comparisons in that poem: both simile and metaphor. Underline them in all your readings (if not with pencil, at least mentally). Note them in conversations, television, sermons . . . whenever you hear words "being put together" . . . be sensitive for this vital tool.

In all of your writing endeavors, ask yourself: "What is this experience, sensation, idea, image . . . *like?*

Can it be expressed best as a comparison?

If so, then should I choose simile or metaphor?

And then work for original use. You'll find it an exciting skill to develop. Here are some of my students' efforts:

The wind throbbed like Tijuana Brass.
The child withered before her glare.

It was as warm as my mother's smile.

The bracelet dangled like a plastic hula hoop on her arm.

His mind gobbled the information.

A peer group is as important to a teen-ager as insulin to a diabetic.

Anger marched onto his face and took control.

The birds formed a church choir in the loft of the trees.

Simile and metaphor is one of the strongest ways of *showing* rather than telling. It is also one of the best means of saying *much* in little. And . . . isn't it an inimitable camera for word pictures?

2. Personification.

Personification may be defined simply as endowing an object or idea with personal characteristics. It really is a special type of metaphor: an implied comparison between the animate and inanimate of our world.

Its problem is the same that Orwell pointed out in regard to metaphor and simile: the cliché, the hackneyed, the common!

You know them:

"The tree lifted its arms."

"The sky smiled."

"The moon looked down."

This is such trite use of personification that a reader is usually turned off. It is best not to use a figure of speech at all . . . unless you can make it throb with originality and new life.

Some of my students' beginning efforts may help stimulate your beginning list:

They laid the baby in the crib's embrace.

His hand on her hair whispered its hymn of love.

The flower kissed her cheek as she knelt in the path.

The wind repulsed my efforts to go home.

The brook laughed at my city shoes.

Personification can be a most meaningful device if you will take the time, and the effort to cultivate its original use. I had never given much thought to personification until this illness has forced me to lie still hour after hour focusing on inanimate objects. And the more I have studied them, the closer I feel to them and understand the effective imagery in personification.

I awoke this morning with swollen face and the beginning of pain. I warily opened one slit of eye in the puff and a bright red rose *waved* and *called to me:* "Cheer up! Cheer up!" And in spite of the marshmallow face and the throbbing physical . . . I laughed. All because an inanimate object, literally for me, "took on animate characteristics" . . . waved . . . and called joy to me!

Personification isn't just a mystical tool to be used by Shakespeare. It's good writing for *you!*

(It can also bring good focus, cheerful messages, joyful triumph over unpleasantness . . . in *living!*)

3. Apostrophe.

Apostrophe is the poetic name for addressing a person or thing . . . present or absent. This takes little discussion to understand and use whenever it fits. You may speak to the moon, to the reader, to a group. . . . It is, very simply, a direct address. "Rise Up, Ye Men of God" is an example from a common hymn. "Starlight, Starbright" is an example from childhood dreams.

4. Synecdoche.

Synecdoche (sah-nak'-doki) is a figure of speech where a part is named instead of the whole. My favorite example of that is a note written by my non-poetic husband who had gone back to the campus where we had both been professors for eight years. Because of my illness, he was alone.

On a sudden impulse, he wrote me a note that read:

"Every corner I turn, I hear your laughter.
My heart cries."

My laughter is only a "part" of the "whole" of the wife he was missing on the familiar campus. But by its specificity, the use of the synecdoche made the note more poignant than had he merely written: "Every corner I turn, I miss you." Also there is synecdoche in the Personification line that follows. He would tell you that his whole being hurt with loneliness. But the expression is more powerful because he selected a "part" to stand for the "whole" and said: "My HEART cries" . . . which is more forceful than saying "All of me cries."

Synecdoche is truly the poetic way of saying, "Prefer the specific to the general word." However you phrase it, it is a strong instrument in communication.

5. Metonymy.

Metonymy (mah-ton'-ah-mi) is using one word which suggests another. The favorite example in a college class of this figure of speech is "Bring Milton to class tomorrow." Unless you know the context, you expect a man, boy, or dog to appear on the next day. What is intended, of course, is that the students bring *Paradise Lost* written by John Milton.

A more apt example is given in a student's Notebook.

"When my sister and I were little, we used to make up a communication network understood only by ourselves. 'Cotton Candy' meant that we would meet in the hall after our parents went to bed. With our pillows and dolls, we would slip down and cuddle in the darkness on the den loveseat and whisper stories. Some of my happiest memories are connotatively wrapped up in the words 'Cotton Candy.' So I use metonymy whenever I write my sister and say: 'Come have Cotton Candy.' I am using a word that suggests much more."

I suggested that my student develop the idea. She wrote a story entitled "Cotton Candy." She read it in class and it became a term that is still used by members of that class. In fact only this week, I received a "Get Well" card from a young attorney and across its panel was scrawled: "When you get better, Jane and I'll fly to Denver for Cotton Candy!"

Some words are built into our language of successful use of Metonymy (e.g., I saw it was her hand—meaning it was her signature, et cetera)—but one of the most effective means of implanting an idea for a reader to remember is to create your own. The entire class of collegians has a special word that means warm and wonderful feelings . . . because a young girl shared an experience of metonymy. If you can do this, it will be a sharing that will be forever remembered. There is an intimacy formed that can come through few other figures of speech . . . when you create your own.

6. Oxymoron.

Oxymoron is not quite as common as metaphor, but a bit less exotic than metonymy. Oxymoron may be defined as combining contradictory words for an unusual effect.

Here are some examples:

Cruel kindness   (Ever seen it or been the recipient? I have!)
Darkness visible   (So black you could actually *see* the black. . . . It's an experience I know!)
Violent peace   (Is that our world today?)
Screaming silence   (Hour after hour in an empty house? Oh yes! It does, sometimes, SCREAM!)

This figure of speech takes special effort, deliberate thought but it *is* a tool for *effective* communication!

7. Litotes.

Litotes states that something is true by denying its opposite.

It is an understatement and my husband is an expert in its use, while it has rarely crossed my tongue. Ask him: "How is your day?" He will reply: "It wasn't bad." So you know it was okay.

When the doctor takes him into the hospital hall and gives him a grave prognosis on my condition, he will return and say: "Things aren't so good." So I know they discussed death.

John Milton was a master of this device. For example, he had Satan strike a pose when he talks about the battle with God and says: "That strife was not inglorious." He means it was, indeed, glorious . . . but he will understate it.

The tool has its unique charm and effect. Consider it. Develop it. Use it when it will best communicate your thought, mood, or reflection.

8. Hyperbole.

Hyperbole is the opposite of litotes. My husband has probably never used it; I use it frequently and enthusiastically! Hyperbole is extravagant exaggeration!

John Donne was a master of hyperbole. One of my favorite examples is when he said he could outdistance the sun in getting to his love because he took "more wings and spurs" than the sun could muster! Now that is *some* statement!

Both litotes and hyperbole are excellent devices for humor. Read Erma Bombeck, Jean Kerr, or your favorite "light" writer and you'll find pages filled with these two figures of speech in effective action. Both are used in serious writing, but should be handled with care. They are both terrific in humor.

9. Epithet.

Epithet is the technical name for the descriptive adjective, noun, or phrase. You learned this elementary tool of description in elementary school, but it is an important figure of speech.

Some examples from collegians' notebooks:

I was hot-chocolate warm.
The dream-filled eyes of the girl stirred my instincts to protect her.
She was flower-beautiful in her dress.
Her china-doll fragility was haunting.
He has inimitable strength.

10. Inversion.

Inversion is a figure of speech which changes the ordinary structure of words so that the most significant part of the sentence, phrase, or paragraph comes first.

Some examples from Notebooks are:

With triumph, I heard the news.
Him I beheld from a distance . . . with longing.
With a dream, I lay me down to sleep.

Home . . . I want to go.
His love I absorbed like a sponge.

Inversion is a simple device . . . but a good one. It spotlights the vital element in a sentence. Be alert to its effective use.

11. Epigram.

An epigram is a figure of speech that phrases an old idea in a fresh manner. It is always concise, usually witty, and often memorable.

EXAMPLES:

If you have no capital, I am glad of it. You don't need capital; you need common sense, not copper cents.

—Russell Conwell

To be as good as our fathers we must be better.

—Wendell Phillips

You need to raise less corn and more hell.

—Mary Elizabeth Lease

An epigram takes real mind-bending effort. When successfully developed, it is inimitable communication.

12. Antithesis.

Antithesis is well-known today because of John Kennedy's Inaugural Address. But it is an old figure of speech that he revived so well. Its definition would simply be: a balanced sentence in which two parts weigh against each other in sharply contrasting an idea.

Here are examples taken from Kennedy's speech:

Let us never negotiate out of fear; but let us never fear to negotiate.

United, there is little we cannot do in a host of cooperative ventures; divided, there is little we can do—for we dare not meet a powerful challenge at odds and split asunder.

And, of course, his most famous:

Ask not what your country can do for you—ask what you can do for your country.

Antithesis is rare because it is difficult. Thought, compression, and imagery are required. But if you have a point you want your reader to remember, antithesis can often be your most effective tool.

13. Rule of Three.

Also called "the Triplet," this is a phenomenon of the English language. It is found that the rhythm of our words, phrases, and even points to be made in a single piece seem to be most impressive when grouped in threes.

EXAMPLES:

We must have faith, courage, and perseverance.
The campaign epithet of 1884 was "Rum, Romanism, and Re-bellion."
There's a majesty about him; there's a halo around him; there's a strength within him.

Note the rhythm in the triplet. It accentuates communication beautifully and enhances content.

14. Parallelism.

Parallelism may be used in many ways: a series of sentences may commence in a similar fashion; a series of sentences may be similar in form; or phrases within a sentence may be parallel.

EXAMPLES:

From John Kennedy's Inaugural Address:
Four successive paragraphs begin with "Let both sides . . ."
He developed another point with these sentence beginnings:
"To those old allies . . .
"To those new states . . .
"To those people in the huts and villages . . .
"To those nations . . ."

From a eulogy on JFK:
By our timidity, we have encouraged the aggressor;
By our paralysis we have given safe conduct to reactionaries;
By our confusion we have promoted the clarity of evil;
By our small prejudices . . . we have prepared the way for
monstrous . . . acts that have betrayed us all.

From Lincoln's Second Inaugural Address:
With malice toward none, with charity for all, with firmness
in the right as God gives us to see the right, let us strive on to
finish the work we are in, to bind up the nation's wounds,
to care for him who shall have borne the battle and for his
widow and his orphan, to do all which may achieve and cherish a just and lasting peace among ourselves with all nations.

Parallelism not only adds impressiveness by repetition, it is
another tool which breathes rhythm, even cadence, into communication that is startlingly effective. It is a tool that requires
conscious effort to develop to skillful use. It is worth the effort.

11

THE SOUND EFFECTS

There are important sound effects that can add color, rhythm, and emphasis to your writing. Use your Notebook to begin internalizing them as you dig into the inner you.

1. Rhyme.

I know this sound effect is generally considered for use only in structured poetry. That does not have to be true. Internal rhyme can add a spotlight of significance and a musical fluidity that can be useful in expression of many ideas in prose.

You may want to write structured poetry in your Notebook. If so, you will certainly want to use rhyme. Your best help will be to secure for your library the book, The Writer's Rhyming Dictionary written by Langford Reed, published by The Writer, Inc., Boston, Massachusetts.

Briefly, you should know that there are six fundamental types of rhyme.

(a)   Masculine rhyme or Stressed rhyme.

EXAMPLES: rake—cake
recline—divine
interrupt—abrupt

(b)   Feminine rhyme or Unstressed rhyme.

    EXAMPLES: fatter—batter

                  daily—gaily

                  reviving—arriving

    (*Note:*   Rhymed stressed syllable followed by identical unstressed syllable.)

(c)   Off rhyme or Slant rhyme.

    EXAMPLES: heel—kill

                  rave—have

                  wind—behind

(d)   Internal rhyme.

    EXAMPLES: As I REVIEWED the situation, the haunting fears PURSUED.

                  My head was bowed as I went to CONFESS for I knew the thunder of his angry REDRESS would crash my hopes.

                  He was UNSWERVING in believing he was DESERVING of punishment.

(e)   Triple rhyme.

    EXAMPLES: Track to me—Back to me

                  Reach afar—Touch a star

                  Give the chance—Live the dance

    (*Note:*   Effective in end rhyme and internal rhyme.)

(f)   Quadruple rhyme.

    EXAMPLES: When you see us—Then you free us

                  You propagate—And regulate

                  I sing a song—Why ring a gong?

2. Alliteration.

This sound effect may be defined as the repetition of the *initial consonant* sounds in phrases or sentences near to each other. This is one of the most beautiful tools for rhythm and artistry.

> EXAMPLES: Your Face will Freeze with the Force of Fear.
>
> I tried to be Straight and Strong and Soldierly . . . and then I Stumbled!
>
> I looked up through My tears and saw him Mirrored in My Mind: Measured, Mentored, Magnified.

(*Note:* The repetitive consonant must be the initial one as is here shown.)

3. Assonance.

This sound effect may be defined as the repetition of *vowel* sounds in phrases or sentences near to each other.

> EXAMPLES: We tAlk and wAlk and tAlk some more.
>
> I lEave the flowers to haunt the prickly wEEds and try to understand their nEEds, the rEasons for their grEEds.
>
> The mOre they outpOur their hearts, the mOre I understand.

4. Consonance.

This sound effect may be defined as the repetition of *consonant* sounds in phrases or sentences near to each other. It need *not* be an initial consonant as in alliteration.

> EXAMPLES: They are Laughing, cLapping, smiLing, backsLapping because they Love Life.
>
> I don't want to waLk or taLk or watch the cLock or staLk a scheduLe.
>
> Don'T you agree a parTiTioned Tower can be comforTing To The Timid, selecT for The eliTe, and sTifling To the personaliTy?

5. Onomatopoeia.

This is a device where the writer creates a word or selects a word that *sounds like* the action or object described.

EXAMPLES: [The ice] CRACKED and GROWLED; and
ROARED and HOWLED. . . .
From: *The Rime of the Ancient Mariner*

SLURP!   BLIP!
TONK!   PFITT!
He GALLUMPHED down the stairs.

Onomatopoeia is your effort to let your reader *hear* for himself rather than your *telling* him *about* the sound. It requires careful creation but is always effective when used with skill.

6. Euphony.

Words that appeal to the eye and/or ear as especially pleasant, even apart from their meaning, is the definition of this sound effect. Lexicographer Wilfred J. Funk lists the following among our most beautiful words . . . which give "euphonious" sound, rhythm, and appeal to our communication.

EXAMPLES: dawn . . . hush . . . lullaby . . .
murmuring . . . tranquil . . . mist . . .
luminous . . . chimes . . . golden . . .
melody . . . tinkling . . . love . . .

7. Cacophony.

This is a sound effect where the writer chooses words of especially UNpleasant sounds. Edgar Allen Poe spoke of the raven as "this grim, ungainly, ghastly, gaunt, and ominous bird of yore," thus giving an excellent illustration of cacophony (and alliteration, if you notice). Other examples of UNpleasant sounding words are:

spinach . . . naughtiness . . . plutocrat . . .
mash . . . sap . . . plump . . . victuals . . .

phlegmatic . . . jazz . . . barren . . . wailing . . .
hate . . . cold . . . fishy . . . clammy . . . death . . .

Like Figures of Speech, the Sound Effects take diligent effort, deliberate energy, demanding earnestness (I'm straining for double alliteration . . . did you note? . . . and also am using a triplet for you to observe . . . but the statement *is* true!) to use with skill.

They provide the sensory immediacy for a reader to best *experience* your communication. They are artists' language brushes with which he may best paint the shades and nuances of word pictures.

An artist works long at a canvas learning basic strokes with various brushes.

The pianist spends hours on finger exercises and scales.

The writer practices in his Notebook fundamental rules, figures of speech, sound effects.

Ultimately the artist paints a masterpiece.

Ultimately the pianist plays "Beethoven's Fifth."

Ultimately the writer communicates with clarity and beauty the record of his own thoughts, feelings, philosophies, experiences . . . in expression of self, in worship of God, in sharing with others! I challenge you to make that last "ultimate" your own!

THE PRINCIPLES

Writing creatively has its own unique principles. Some are the same as journalistic reporting. Some are the exact opposite. I will try to state these fundamentals as concisely as possible.

1. Vigorous Compression.

The creative writer should use every device discussed to this point as graphically as possible, for most of these tools will enable one to use the fewest words possible. A good principle is: Say *much* in *little*. Communicate the greatest number of ideas in the smallest amount of space. This is no call for incomplete work, it *is* a call for complete work done with such thoroughness that it is "right." There is no slack in the writing.

Beginning writers have a tendency to verbal bombast. One of my students turned in this breathtaking example:

"At this moment in my life, I am standing stock still for a long soul-searching second in the midst of a reeling, wheeling world to search my soul as to what this great gigantic universe in which I find myself really is, what its true meaning of existential reality may be, and toward what farflung unknown destiny it is tending its way." WHEWWWW!!!!

You're probably never guilty of THAT much wordiness, but the disease may be beginning; it is insidious; so watch for it.

That is why the Haiku is such an important part of learning how to write. It focuses on vigorous words and tight compression.

2. Climax.

In journalism, you state the most important first; the details follow. Not so in writing creatively.

To create climax, you build in a steadily increasing power structure to the important point you want to make. The least important point is always made *first;* the most important made *last.* This is true in sentences, paragraphs, entire pieces of writing.

3. Nouns and Verbs Carry the Heavy Load.

Mark Twain wrote: "When in doubt, omit the adjective."
Emerson advised, "Let the noun be self-sufficient."

You may note he used an adjective in his admonition, but it is an important principle that when nouns and verbs *can* bear the weight of expression alone, it is usually your best writing. "She was a tiny girl" has not the power of "She was an elf." "We could see the splitting lightning in the sky" is not as strong as "The lightning split the sky before our eyes."

Sprinkle your writing with adjectives sparingly; go heavy on the nouns and verbs.

4. Proportion.

It is a general principle that should be rarely broken: ideas should be treated with length concurrent with their importance. Since the least important ideas come first and the most important last, most creative manuscripts should look like a pyramid.

As in all principles, there are exceptions.

One of the most notable in literature is the succinct word picture: "Jesus wept." It is so powerful that it stands alone. Any other details or exposition building to it or coming from it would be extraneous. Man stands in wonder at the image of the God-man crying for His friend, sharing human sorrow. "Building" is not necessary.

Such effective human brevity, however, can be used only on

special occasions for special effects. Consider well before breaking fundamental rules or principles.

5. Repetition.

Henry James said: "The good expositor should choose key words and play upon them." That is true not only of words, but of phrases and ideas. You will find that carefully placed repetition is useful for giving emphasis to your point . . . for giving unity to your entire manuscript . . . for giving clarity so that the referent is always apparent . . . for giving coherence and all-round effectiveness to your communication.

Several years ago, I wrote a book entitled *No Matter the Weather*. Its point was single: The Presence of God will be with His earthly child *No Matter the Weather*. To emphasize that point, I used the phrase at the conclusion of each section of the book. The repetition also gave "unity" to the whole and made crystal-clear the "referent" (the point of the book) all through the reading. I believe it was one of the most useful principles used to make that book cohesive in content with an "all-round effectiveness."

When I first gained consciousness after a severe crisis in my illness, I understood, truly for the first time, that life would have to change for me. My husband was sitting by my bed. I whispered my confession; he grabbed my hand and said: "Oh honey, I know. We'll find another way to live." And, in awe at such love, I whispered: "You would love me . . . EVEN THOUGH?" In tears, he responded: "EVEN THOUGH."

Those two words now are used repeatedly in my communication with him about my feelings ("Thank you for loving me . . . EVEN THOUGH!")

my changing philosophies   ("I see now [some specific] is not as important as I thought; I'll learn to be happy . . . EVEN THOUGH!")

my adjustments to the illness   ("I woke up today and heard my heart say: Thank You, God, for LIFE . . . EVEN THOUGH!")

In the repetition of those two words, there is a clarity of understanding between writer and reader that would take paragraphs,
even pages, to completely spell out. In addition to the force of
repetition in giving emphasis, unity, and cohesion, it can also
be vital in compression: saying *much* in *little*.

Repetition of structure is also an important principle. The
above discussion was of specific words. But you can take a
certain rhythm of language and use it repeatedly for effect. An
example in a sentence would be: "The race is not to the swift,
nor the battle to the strong, nor bread to the wise, nor riches
to men of understanding, nor favor to men of skill." That same
kind of rhythmic repetition can be used for larger elements such
as paragraphs, sections, chapters . . . just as I used repetition of
No Matter the Weather (a specific phrase) in the book.

More examples of structural repetition may be seen in excerpts
from the Kennedy and Lincoln inaugurals presented in the chapter on figures of speech. Especially note those dealing with
parallelism.

6. Suspense.

Three things comprise suspense: a hint, a wait, a fulfillment.
The hint may be either an open statement such as: "I shall tell
you how Dorothy Thumrod murdered her son and remained out
of prison" . . . or by a vague suggestion such as "It was rumored
that her child did not die of pneumonia. . . ."

The wait is composed of the events leading to the fulfillment.
An example of suspense-building would be: (1) He wanted to
be a lawyer but always felt a haunting sense of doom. (2) He
went to law school and made good grades. (3) He sacrificed
everything for study and financing his dream pursuit. (4) The
names of those passing the bar exam are posted. His name heads
the list. (5) On the way to read the list, he is killed by a speed-
ing car.

Mystery writers are good sources to study the elements of
suspense-building in the most obvious form. Read a few of these
and note their use of the three elements: when, where, how do
they give the hint; what is the structure of their building through
the wait . . . to fulfillment? That answer will give you your best
guide to follow.

7. Directness.

One of the marks of a good writer is his ability to state graphically and explicitly his ideas. One way to achieve this is to work, as a general habit, with short, though strong, words.

A poll of writers indicated the percentage of their work that was limited to words of *one syllable*. It looked like this:

Somerset Maugham	75%	Thomas B. Macaulay	70%
Katherine Mansfield	74%	R. L. Stevenson	71%
John Galsworthy	70%	Charles Dickens	73%
Willa Cather	69%	Walter Pater	65%
Sinclair Lewis	78%	Matthew Arnold	66%

Surprising, isn't it? A wide, effective vocabulary obviously can still be simple and direct.

Another way to achieve directness is to be sensitive to jargon . . . which is straining for figurative language to the point of losing meaning in the words. The "jargoneer" would never say directly "he was born"; he would say: "He first saw the light of day" or "He gave his first yell as a living soul" or "He first gazed upon the human condition"! Figurative language is effective, as we have discussed, but it should be used sensibly, carefully, and at the right time.

Speak simply, directly, concisely. Use figures of speech in a straightforward manner . . . never when it smacks of "bombast" or wordiness . . . or language contrived. This is essential for the best communication.

8. Symbolism.

A symbol is defined as "something that stands for or represents another thing; especially, an object used to represent something abstract; e.g. the dove is a symbol of peace; the cross is the symbol of Christianity; the star is a symbol of Judaism." A good writer will become a "symbolist" who is "a person who uses symbols in representing ideas."

Symbolism is difficult unless the writer works carefully for clarity and consistency. I know many mystical writers use symbolism in a highly intellectual, deliberately ambiguous way, and it is praiseworthy for the intelligentsia. But if you are writing in an effort to share with yourself and with others like you, you would do well (in my view) to strive for symbolism that is clearly meaningful rather than so ambiguous it demands study and scholarly analysis to understand.

Because much symbolism is difficult to grasp, many beginning writers make no effort to utilize it. I think that is a mistake. You should not overlook the power this tool can have in simplistic use.

You can begin working with symbolism by thinking of concrete things that *do* stand for abstract ideas or feelings for *you*. When I began such exploration, I immediately thought of roller skates. An ill-matched pair of roller skates is (to me) a symbol of love.

Let me explain.

When I was about six years of age, all of my group of friends mounted skates and the world moved on silvery wheels. Oh, how I longed for a pair of skates of my very own. But my father was the minister of a small parish that paid a small salary and I was the youngest of eight children. So I never mentioned my desire for skates. I understood there was room for no such luxuries in our budget.

But my father observed my intense desire and began to seek a way to satisfy it. So through attic, garage, and junk heap, my father looked for an answer to my prayer. One day he came upon an old skate that was rusty red from age and lack of use. This, he presented to me and, in greatest jubilation, I skated on my one rusty skate for several weeks.

Later, my father found another skate. This was silvery, like those of my friends, but it didn't have any clamps to hold it on my foot. Undaunted, my father made a strap to hold the skate on my foot . . . and, feeling like the Queen of Sheba, I sailed forth on my two *wonderful* skates! The rusty one was too short for my foot; the silvery one was too long . . . but they skated fine!

Someone once asked me when I told this story as an adult if I hadn't been embarrassed about my skates. I was horrified at the thought. Ashamed of my skates? Why, they were my most cherished possession, for they were a gift from my father's heart. No girl ever cherished a pair of skates more than I did those ill-matched, ill-fitting skates my father gave to me.

Think through your life. What tangible objects symbolize love for you? Christmas trees symbolize joy for me . . . don't they for you? Gingerbread men symbolize caring companionship around a kitchen table . . . remember? Begin making a list of the concrete items in *your* life that represent the intangible.

When my husband was critically ill, I grabbed an envelope from the trash can in his hospital room and scribbled on it these words. Note the use of the symbol.

> The world has stilled.
> The carousel has stopped.
> No more sound of tinkling music;
> No more kaleidoscope of bright dizzy colors;
> The world sits on its axis;
> The carousel poises on its platform
> Waiting
> Tensely
> Prayerfully
> Lovingly
> For you.

I challenge you to begin identifying symbols in your life; practice their usage in Notebook work; *use* them in your writing to those important people in your life to whom the symbol would be the *most* meaningful.

9. Atmosphere.

The dictionary definition of this common term is "the general effect produced by specific features, e.g. restaurant atmosphere." The more literary definition is "the general tone of a work of art: as a play with a fateful atmosphere." Both are relevant for our consideration.

For your reader to *experience* with you, he will need to sense, feel, understand the exact "atmosphere" or the "general effect produced by specific features" of the setting to truly be a part. From your skill in presenting "atmosphere" comes the "general tone" of your work.

When I was in graduate school, my class was challenged by a professor to identify a list of questions which would guide the writer to the creation of atmosphere. He felt such specificity would make the task easier. I agree with him.

I make the same challenge to you.

You will probably add to the list, but here are some of the questions you should ask when you set about the job of creating "atmosphere" in your writing.

1.   What objects do you see? What is their arrangement? (This is the very simple, but vital, beginning. When I presented this principle in my college-teaching, I would take students on field trips. One class hour we would spend inside a church; the next class hour, we would spend in a family den; the next class period we would spend in the waiting room or "parlor" of a funeral home, et cetera. Each was a *totally* different atmosphere. Immediately you can see the importance of the writer sharing the "feel" of the church, the den, the funeral parlor with the reader . . . because the "mood" . . . even the content of the communication is "colored" . . . changed because of atmosphere. I urge you to try this same exercise in as many diverse settings as you can. And the way to begin is to simply look about and begin to note specific objects and arrangements, e.g. the church: the stained glass window, the sun streaming through, the cross, the altar, the organ all arranged for a unified "picture" of worship; the den: the fireplace, the rocking chair where the mother sat watching the baby hurling plastic toys across the room all cohesed in a unified "picture" of family; the funeral parlor: bland pictures on the wall; upright sofas set about; tables empty except for boxes of Kleenex all arranged in a cold, awkward, unfamiliar pattern which emphasized the cold, awkward, unfamiliar emotions that were exposed in the room. The first question will easily begin your search for "atmosphere"; the others will lead you into full exploration; from this knowledge will come your skill in presenting "atmosphere" in your writing.)

2.   Will figures of speech (e.g. metaphor, simile) assist you in scene description?

3.   What objects are stationary? What objects move? How? Why? Is there any arrangement to the movement?

4.   Describe the colors. Can you use figures of speech here?

5.   If sunlight is a part of the scene, how does it affect the objects, the motion, the colors?

6. If there is no sunlight, describe the source and quality of light and its resulting effects.

7. What about the noise level? How can you describe the noise? Is there an arrangement to the sounds?

8. Is sound a dominant part of the creation of atmosphere? If so, how? Why?

9. Is smell a dominant part of the creation of atmosphere? If so, how? Why?

10. Is taste a dominant part of the atmosphere? If so, what taste? Why? Is this pleasant or unpleasant?

11. Is the texture of objects in the scene significant? Describe.

12. Is the temperature of the scene significant? Describe.

13. Is there a feeling of moisture in the scene? Describe.

14. Is there an extra-sensory feeling in the scene? If so, how do you account for it?

15. Does the scene change your mood in any way? How? Why?

In your Notebook work, strive to "capture" atmosphere of as many diverse places as possible. This will enable you to become a master of this principle which is an imperative in good writing.

10. Poetic License.

This may be defined as a "pact" between the writer and his reader that permits him to depart from rules, conventions, or even factual accuracy to achieve a specific goal. This involves the specifics of syntax, spelling, arrangement, and punctuation, or it can include content when objectivity is sublimated to subjectivity to produce original combinations or fresh contexts.

An example of breaking rules to make a point may be seen in this short piece of free verse I wrote years ago:

God . . .
Life gets so
BUSYBUSYBUSYBUSYBUSYBUSYBUSYBUSYBUSY-
BUSYBUSYBUSYBUSY
That I forget
I need You.

Sometimes
You
Have to trip
Me
So that I
  F
   A
    L
     L
      F L A T. . . . .

Then
I remember
I need You.

Forgive.

An example of poetic license in content would be a play I wrote a few years ago in which the adulteress whom Jesus met at the Well of Samaria moves to Jerusalem as His follower. She became close friends with Stephen, the young leader of the fledgling church, and his brother. In the play, she was a vital participant in events following the stoning of Stephen.

When theologians were checking the play content for accuracy, this was a problem because there is the general assumption that the woman at the well was young . . . and I pictured her as middle-aged at the time of Stephen's death. There is no evidence to indicate that the woman ever saw Jesus after the confrontation at the well.

But . . . poetic license "won the day" because these assumptions could not be proven false. It *could* have happened just that way. And, in developing the content in that manner, an unusual context could be set in which important truths could be dramatized.

One thing about poetic license difficult for my collegians to grasp is that . . . before you break a rule, however, you have to *know* the rule! Your breaking is done for a deliberate effect.

Especially in writing free verse, my students would hotly debate the point that learning metrical patterns (not used per se

in free verse) was important. My contention was that learning the
metrical patterns gave a solidity of rhythm to free verse that
could come no other way. Understanding and feeling the solid
rhythmical patterns gave the poet a knowledge, a feel that made
his breaking the rules meaningful. Without such knowledge, without such disciplined background, your efforts can become slapdash.

So poetic license is not a freedom to ignore convention. It is
merely an understanding that you can do so for a desired effect.
Utilize it in both poetry and prose when it will enhance your
communication.

11. Revision.

One of the major problems with beginning writers (as has been
stated in another chapter) is their satisfaction with first efforts.
For some reason, the art of writing has the reputation that it
comes easily. I remember how shocked I was one evening when,
at a wedding shower, the hostess came over and asked if I could
write and give a poem. I guess I looked at her blankly, for she
said: "Oh, I know these things just flow off the top of your head
at a moment's notice." Her smile was ingratiating. "Don't you
feel a poem . . . coming on?"

Rather than disillusion the lady, I did perform something I had
written for another wedding shower that "fit" the occasion, but I
have never quite recovered from the shock of her assumption that
my craft "just flowed off the top of my head at a moment's notice!" If I had the urge to heal people, this lady would assume that
I would have thorough training and practice. But for producing a
poem, it just had to "come on!"

One of the reasons for this fallacy is that so many of the
masters never took advanced courses in writing, but that does not
mean that they did not study their art intensely. In fact, many of
them such as Ben Johnson, Henry James, T. S. Eliot, and others
have written prolifically about techniques and principles of writing. A college course, or a professional guide, simply gives you
the shortcuts the masters discovered the hard way. But whether
involved in structured study (as a medical student is) or not, a

writer must study just as hard and know his art just as thoroughly.

I remember one young man who listened patiently to my lectures on figures of speech, sound effects, and principles of writing. After class one day, he came and said patronizingly: "Of course, you really don't believe we will go to all that trouble in our writing!" His look turned to astonishment when I replied: "That depends on whether you want to be a writer or a hack!" There simply is no way to write well without learning the rules and being willing, then, to polish and revise and repolish to gain the best phrasing and expression possible. And if you aren't excited and interested in the development and use of the *processes* of writing: the juggling of all the elements that go into effective expression . . . you would probably be happier cutting grass. You have to love words . . . and their arrangements . . . and their potentials . . . to "go to all that trouble" . . . but when such love is yours, you'll find the rules and the principles seductive and irresistible.

Many try to cop out on revision by maintaining that this deletes the effects of inspiration and spontaneity. That *is* a cop-out! Most of inspiration is hard work; and the flashes that do come in spontaneity are easily retained. Most memorable writing has been altered and refined by careful, caring authors. "The coming of the Muse" is, for the most part, poetic nonsense. If you want to write well, you have to write and write and write and write and write and write and . . . until you have it as perfectly as you can get it. You would expect to play and play and play and play and play and . . . before you performed a Chopin concerto. The principle is equally true in good writing.

The former managing editor of *Time,* Otto Fuerbringer, wrote that you could tell a good story or a good issue by the amount of good material thrown away. A special speaker at a writer's seminar at my university was discussing his best-selling book. He said that it was written from twenty-three two-inch notebooks, all of his Journals, and about three hundred pages of specifically researched material. He said: "It takes thirty gallons of sap to make a gallon of maple syrup; it takes hundreds of pages of notes to make one *Reader's Digest* article."

Revision is an essential of good writing.

12. Imagination.

Joseph Conrad wrote in 1912: "Only in men's imagination does every truth find an effective and undeniable existence. Imagination, not invention, is the supreme master of art as life."

The dictionary definition of imagination is (a) the act or power of forming mental images of what is not actually present, (b) the act or power of creating mental images of what has never been actually experienced, or of creating new images or ideas by combining previous experiences; creative power. Imagination is often regarded as the more seriously and deeply creative faculty, which perceives the basic resemblances between things, as distinguished from fancy, the lighter and more decorate faculty, which perceives superficial resemblances.

Think of the wisest people you know. Are they not those who think symbolically, who perceive likenesses in things diverse? These are persons who have allowed their unfettered, winging imaginations to aid their expression of concepts or perceptions.

This principle, then, is a wilful jump into this personal intuition, in the Conradian sense, as the fountainhead for writing that attempts to effectively portray the human condition. Writing *is* an effort to share new perceptions of the *facts* of *truth*.

If imagination is a unique personal intuition, then the best stories are within. That is why the Journal is so essential for the writer, if he is to *honestly* examine *truth* in his writings, he has to do so with the uniqueness of his own understanding, his own experiences, his own feelings . . . even though that involves confronting terrifying fear-enshrouded closets. R. V. Cassill wrote that the choice of becoming a writer is the choice to *face some fears!*

It would seem that our personal horrors, our personal dark corners, our personal unsolved problems are arenas that we must explore and come to terms with. And in the coping with these areas, along with the happinesses, of course, we find the springing fountain of our imagination. And from this source come stories that no one else could ever write, because they come from the peculiarity of self!

You are a once-in-a-lifetime, never-before-on-earth, never-to-be-again personality. Understand the importance of that. Then

through the activity of imagination (the perception of relationships), gowned in the garments of fiction, you give birth to
your story. And it will be a story that, if you are truly honest,
could have come from no one in all the world . . . but *you!* And
from that uniqueness will come a shaft of light, a way of looking
at things, a key to Truth that is your own gift to everyone else.

It does not matter whether you are writing autobiography or
not. The point of your story is your unique "world view" . . .
your personal manner of understanding, a fresh way of looking at
life, brought out in the form of a story or poem or illustration for
yourself and others to perceive.

And, while we're on this subject, let it be said that the truly
dramatic adventures of your life are less likely to stimulate stories. One of my professors used to say: "The best stories lie in the
valleys of life, in the mundane commonplace where a writer can
find the wonder of Truth even there!" The Journal and the Notebook are two excellent places to develop imagination. Remember
that image and imagination are related words. Stretch your *images* into *imagination* for we tend to think first in images . . .
then in words.

Some suggestions for practice is to take your Notebook and listen to a recording. First listen quietly with eyes and Notebook
closed. Then try to capture the emotions of the music in imaginative words. Do the same with pictures. Movies are available at
your local library or free from the Telephone Company of majestic scenery with musical background. There, in a world without
words, strive to impress the images so firmly on your mind that
your imagination can play with them until they transport you into
a new visual world.

To underline the importance of this principle for the writer
wanting to write for self-expression, for God worship and God
service, for sharing with others, Clyde S. Kilby has written the
following essay entitled "Christian Imagination." Let me share it
with you.

I want to base what I have to say on three facts which I
think indisputable.

The first is that the Bible belongs to literature; that is, it is
a piece of art. Does it make any difference that the Book we

look upon as holy comes to us in literary form rather than in the form of abstract doctrine or systematic theology? Is the poetry of the Bible a statement of fact plus an artistic decoration? If we summarize the Twenty-third Psalm to declare that God cares for His children as a good shepherd cares for his sheep, do the poetry and the prose summary amount to the same thing? If so, why the poetry in the first place? What change takes place when a piece of poetry is turned into a piece of doctrine or of practical exhortation?

How is the divine inspiration of the Bible related to the great oddity that the longest of the Psalms was written in the form of an acrostic? Was the acrostic form from God or only from the poet? The best authority I know of on the Bible as literature, Richard G. Mouton, points out the large variety of literary forms in the Scripture—epic cycles, orations, dramatic anthems, war anthems, festal hymns, litanies, acrostics, elegies, national anthems, odes, sonnets, epigrams, rhapsodies, vision cycles, encomiums, and so forth. Did God inspire the form or only the content of the Bible? Is its form only a man-made incidental? Should Christian teachers ever encourage students to read the Bible as literature?

I recall, as a young teacher, going to the president of my college and asking him if I might safely say in chapel that the Bible is often figurative in its language. (He promptly answered in the affirmative.) Why the "indirection" of [the simile] that a godly man is like a tree planted by the rivers of water, and the extreme exaggeration [hyperbole] of saying that the floods and the trees of the field clap their hands and sing? Are such expressions to be dismissed as mere adornments, embroidery, as feathers—perhaps very pretty ones—that are to be removed from the turkey before its caloric and real meaning can come into existence?

Why isn't the Bible plain, expository, concrete? Why those numerous and difficult paradoxes flung at the reader, such as Jeremiah 17:9—"The heart is deceitful above all things, and desperately wicked," and Romans 10:10—"With the heart man believeth unto righteousness?" Why the oddity of Paul's prayer in Ephesians 3:19, that Christians may know the love of God which passeth knowledge, or of He-

brews 4:11, "Labor . . . to enter . . . into rest," and the
frequent wordplay even in our Lord's own language? All of
which suggests the literary quality of the Bible.

The second indisputable fact is that, because one . . . and
possibly the greatest . . . ingredient of literature is imagination, we must say that the Bible is an imaginative book.
There is no literature without imagination—strong, honest,
often daring imagination.

The third indisputable fact is that the greatest artist of all,
the greatest imaginer of all, is the one who appears at the
opening of Genesis. Esthetics has to do with form, design,
harmony, beauty. Perhaps the key word is "form." Now the
earth, says Genesis, was without form. God shaped the creation into form—light and darkness, the heavens, the teeming
waters, the multitudinous fauna and flora. He shaped birds
and roses and morning glories and dandelions, the hippo
and the alligator, the mammoth and the giraffe, and man in
his own image. And we are told that he looked upon each
thing he had shaped and saw that it was good. The whole he
saw to be "very good." Even after the fall of man, the Bible
treats nature as beautiful, with God as its maker and
wielder. Job, the Psalms, and numerous other books celebrate—perhaps to a point a bit scary to some Christians—
the intimate relationship of God and His creation. God did
not, as so many of us, think that the esthetic was an incidental for leisure time.

And we can also add that God is an architect. The Scripture tells us in no uncertain detail that God put his spirit
into the workmen who built Solomon's temple and that it
required seventy thousand men to bear burdens and eighty
thousand to hew timbers in the mountains, with thirty-three
hundred supervisors, over a period of seven years. It is alto-
gether proper, I think, to imagine God telling Solomon how
to carve the magnificent lilies to go at the top of the great
columns. More glorious still is the final fulfillment God
promises in Ephesians 1 where he says (Philips' translation): "He purposes in His sovereign will that all human
history shall be consummated in Christ, that everything that
exists in heaven or earth shall find its perfection and

fulfillment in Him." No greater esthetic consummation is possible.

Now when we look from these three facts to contemporary evangelical Christianity, we find a great oddity. The people who spend the most time with the Bible are in large numbers the "foes" of art and the sworn foes of imagination. And I grow in the feeling that these people have quite an astonishing indifference to the created world. Evangelicals hear the great "I Am" of God but they are far less aware of the "I Am" of His handiwork. Furthermore, when evangelicals dare attempt any art form, it is generally badly done.

One cannot escape the fact that many evangelicals, had they the chance, would create a different world and write a different Bible from the ones we have. An article in *His* magazine recently tried to suggest what an evangelical publisher might have done with the manuscript of the Bible. He would have changed all its poetry to good plain prose, removed most of the figures of speech, re-written the parables to make them clearer, taken out the Song of Solomon and such accounts as that of David's relations with Bathsheba and her husband, and kept the whole Bible far simpler—or even reduced it to a numbered set of rules and regulations.

As to the evangelical's skittishness toward imagination, I have looked into the Scriptures and I cannot find such a prejudice there. One prominent evangelical holds that the triad of truth-goodness-beauty is Greek in origin and the Hebrew concept is only that of the true and the holy. I doubt it. I doubt it primarily because of the glorious beauty I see every day in God's handiwork. But I also doubt it from looking at the Scripture. The Revised Standard Version shows ninety uses of the words beauteous, beautiful, beautify and beauty (The King James Version uses seventy-six of these words), and overwhelmingly in a favorable sense. I see no esthetic difference between God's world and His creative work. Even if His world were purely a functional one, the bee and the flower around which it buzzes would be equally glorious, equally fantastic, equally miraculous.

How can it be that with a God Who created birds and the blue of the sky, and Who before the foundation of the

world, wrought out a salvation more romantic than Cin-
derella, with a Christ Who encompasses the highest heaven
and deepest hell, with the very hairs of our heads numbered,
with God closer than hands and feet, Christians often turn
out to have an unenviable corner on the unimaginative and
the commonplace? God shamelessly flings out the rainbow,
but some Christians paint the bumpers of their autos black
or shun attractive clothing, apparently on the ground that
whatever is shiny is sinful. An evangelical sees a picture of a
mission board and writes a warning against the worldliness
that is creeping in because some of the members have hand-
kerchiefs tucked in their coat pockets. Yet when the Lord
talks of espousing Israel (Ezekiel 16:10ff), he says, "I
clothed you with embroidered cloth . . . I swathed you in
fine linen and covered you with silk. And I decked you with
ornaments, and put bracelets on your arms, and a chain on
your neck. And I put . . . earrings in your ears, and a beautiful crown upon your head . . . you were decked with gold
and silver; and your raiment was of fine linen, and silk, and
embroidered cloth."

Evangelical Christians have had one of the purest of mo-
tives and one of the worst of outcomes. The motive is never
to mislead by the smallest fraction of an iota in the precise
nature of salvation, to live it and state it in its utter purity.
But the unhappy outcome has too often been to elevate the
clichér. The motive is that the Gospel shall not be misunder-
stood, nor sullied, nor changed in jot or tittle. The outcome
has often been merely the reactionary, static and hackneyed.

Take evangelical poetry as an example. Some years ago, I
sent an inquiry to Christian editors. The all but unanimous
response was that they published little or no poetry because
what they received was simply trash. The same is more or less
true of all our other creative efforts. I had given up the hope
of ever seeing an evangelical novel that had any artistic merit
when I came upon Olov Hartman's *The Holy Masquerade*.
When I began to praise it, someone asked me if the author
really were an evangelical! I don't know.

But to come a little closer to home, it appears that the
cliché has marked the evangelical's creative efforts because

it first marked his thought and life. C. S. Lewis talks about the child who, on Easter morning, was heard whispering to himself: "Chocolate eggs and Jesus risen." In our desperate evangelical desire for a clear, logical depiction of Jesus risen, we have tended to remove the chocolate eggs. P. T. Forsyth describes the glory and expectation that permeated early Christianity when, as he says, "Life received a horizon in place of a boundary. The Christian Faith introduced the witness of the true Infinite, not a mere mathematical infinity or extension, nor dynamical infinity of energy, but the Infinite of spiritual thought, passion, purpose, and power—the thought and purpose of God, the passion of His holy redeeming love, and the power of the Holy Ghost."

For this expectant and viable Christianity, we have somehow come to elevate the trite and the static as our rule. Our efforts to keep the Gospel pure and the way of salvation clear have led us almost exclusively to the expository, frontal, exegetical, functional, and prosaic. We want the Word of God and everything pertaining to Christianity to be as simple as two times two, yet over against this stands the Bible itself as example, I believe, of another sort of thing.

There is a simplicity which diminishes and a simplicity which enlarges, and evangelicals have too often chosen the wrong one. The first is that of the cliché—simplicity with mind and heart removed. The other is that of art. The first falsifies by its exclusions, the second encompasses. The first silently denies the multiplicity and grandeur of creation, salvation, and indeed, all things. The second symbolizes and celebrates them. The first tries to take the danger out of Christianity and with the danger often removes the actuality. The second suggests the creative and sovereign God of the universe with Whom there are no impossibilities. The contrast suggests that *not* to imagine is what is sinful!

13

THE LAND

Everything we have discussed to this point has been work within yourself. There has been no real discussion of bringing a piece of writing to fulfillment as a full-blown entity that could be shared with others.

The reason for that is the order of things.

A writer, no matter how talented, can never be at his best until he has explored his inner domain; until he has become "Expert in Home-cosmography"; until he has thoroughly tilled and planted his inner land.

Before we turn our attention to the basic principles for writing finished manuscripts to share with others . . . I'd like for us to clearly summarize the elements involved in attaining expertise in "Home-cosmography" or finding one's inner land.

It begins at birth and continues until death. And it is uniquely your own.

It is all the love you have known . . . it is all the hate.

It is all the laughter you have shouted . . . it is all the tears shed.

It is all the applause you have enjoyed . . . it is all the rejection you have endured.

It is all the inspiration received . . . it is all the depression borne.

It is the people in your world. . . .

It is the stories you have read, seen, or imagined. . . .

It is the music you have made a part of self. . . .

It is all the beauty you have known . . . it is all the ugliness.

It is all the privileges granted you . . . it is all the privations
assigned.

It is all the warmth in which you snuggled . . . it is all the
cold in which you shivered.

It is all the bright colors irradiating . . . it is all the Stygian
black enshrouding.

It is the animals you have loved. . . .

It is the clothes you have worn. . . .

It is the art you have admired. . . .

It is the texture

of *you* . . .

one-of-a-kind
never-before-on-earth
never-to-be-again. . . .

It is your unique inner land.

In this soil, your thoughts will take seed.

From this rich substance will come the shape of your ideas

the development of your
characters
the unrolling of your plots.

No one else can write your essays
your poetry
your fiction.

No one else can . . .

because your "Home-cosmography" is peculiarly
your own. It is meshed of all experiences, influences, observations, philosophies, emotions, ideologies that have touched your
life . . . and your response to them.

This mixture composes your inner land. From it will come
your creative expression.

I know.

It is easy to peruse the above and nod in agreement. Of course,
there is an "inner land" which is the essence of self.

But now that you perceive its existence . . . there is more!

It is not enough to understand "Home-cosmography." We must constantly enlarge our "expertise."

It is not enough to recognize our "inner land." We need to till it with care.

How?

Through the *awareness* of life; through recording it, assimilating it for creative *use*.

Through living "with the skin off" . . . and storing life's varied experiences in Journal, file folder, or memory cell.

The word I have used in self-dialogue is: *Know!*

My first memory of it comes at the age of nine. My handsome, brown-eyed brother, Joe, had been fighting in World War II. I understood little of war, but I sensed my parents' anxiety. I felt my own loneliness for his smile.

One usual afternoon, I came home from school. When I entered the living room, I saw, framed in the kitchen doorway, a tall, tanned soldier. I gasped, eyes wide, and then took a flying leap into the strong circle of his arms. My tears mingled with his as he crushed me to his heart.

He turned, still holding me, to Mother and Daddy who arm-circled both of us. All the cold gnawing heart-fear fled before the rushing flood of loving gratitude binding the four of us together. The house was warm, bright, and very full. I remember whispering to myself: *"Know, Ruth. Know."*

Even as a child, I understood that this moment held a richness that would color all my tomorrows. No matter how desolate might be future circumstance, there was this moment when I experienced joy unspeakable and full of glory.

I didn't write it in a Journal then. But I internalized it. It is a vital element in my inner land.

There have been so many. . . .

There was the night I was sixteen and went sleigh riding in the snow . . . my heart whispered at the sparkling wonder: *Know!*

There was the night I was a bride in white lace and satin. I walked down the aisle, placed my hand in Bill's as he sang: "Because God made thee mine, I'll cherish thee . . ." and my heart whispered: *Know!*

There were the moments when I held Billy and Ron for the

first time . . . their solemn eyes studying me . . . and I whispered: "Ruth, *Know!*"

Those moments of wonder splash all through the texture of my land.

There are others.

I remember, as a child, going with my father to visit a parishioner. Glass was broken out of the house windows and rags were stuffed in the frames to keep out the cold. There was one kerosene stove in the drafty house around which huddled the entire family.

I remember one child who came to me to touch my red coat. Her nose was running down over her upper lip, and she gave the discharge a tentative lick with her tongue. I stared at her taut face and sickened at its whitish-blue color which reminded me of skimmed milk.

It was my first exposure to real poverty, to real need. And my heart whispered: *Know!*

"Internalize the ugliness that life can be; feel the cold; try to share in the hunger of this room . . . not merely food hunger . . . but life hunger."

That picture is vividly in my mind now. I can still sense the hunger as a live thing, darting about the room, sucking courage and strength like a weasel. It is a part of my "inner land." Forever. I learned starkly that life is not all dreams-come-true when a brother comes home from war . . . life is also existence-with-no-hope portrayed in the family huddled by the fire, the little girl who hungered to touch my red coat.

There have been so many. . . .

There was the night I was eighteen and two college youth exploded in a violent fight. They screamed at each other as they swung punches. One finally landed squarely and the victim took a few running steps toward where I stood watching . . . and then slumped at my feet in a pool of blood. I was mesmerized as my mind slowly intook the results of anger allowed to erupt in violence. And my heart whispered: *"Know!"*

There was the time, as an adult, when I observed a man of authority crush the career of another to advance his own. My whole being sickened as I whispered: *"Know!"*

Those moments of disenchantment splash all through the texture of my land.

Those are the extremes.

Meshed in between are the ordinary, usual routines that equally help form our land. One must, even in the dusty daily, *know*.

Some of these are:

Reading *Huckleberry Finn* . . . or *Pilgrim's Progress*.
Seeing Julie Andrews in *The Sound of Music*.
A red tricycle. A blue bicycle.
The first velvet dress. The first tuxedo. The first kiss.
The first prayer in the morning. The last dream at night.
Water-skiing. Roller-skating. Surfboarding.
Family. Friends. Teachers. Ministers.
A week in New York City. A month on the farm.
A wedding ring. Little children's laughter.
A house. A piano. A set of china. A gold clock.
Heart-sharing over frosty Cokes. . . .

Know!

Each of these elements, and myriads more, are part and parcel of the reality of *you!*

Know! Record. Assimilate.

For all of your writing will be rooted in . . . will stem from . . . this inner land.

I grew up on the tumbleweed-covered plains of Texas, went to graduate school on the wheat-covered plains of Kansas, and taught college on the wind-swept plains of Oklahoma. When we moved to Colorado, I thought I had been transplanted to another universe. I had never seen such majesty as the Rocky Mountain beauty.

As soon as I could get my house in reasonable order, I drove out to spend an afternoon *knowing* . . . recording . . . assimilating. I took a small spiral notebook on which I had tied a pencil with string. I could make illegible notes to stimulate my memory later.

The morning after my visit to the mountains, I rolled a sheet of paper into the typewriter and let my fingers fly in the recording, assimilating of the *knowing* experience. This is top-of-the-head recounting of elements in my "inner land."

Let me share a part of it with you.

I rubbed my eyes.

They ached from staring at this brilliantly colored, wildly beautiful, incredibly diverse landscape.

To my right, the mountains joined hands circling, tier on tier, in a savage challenging dance. There were glowing rings of the dancer's colors: pink, maroon, scarlet, striped white and gray. In formation, the colors dipped, gyrated, pirouetted as if to the beat of rousing drums.

My breath caught in my throat as I turned to view, below me, a stream glimmering like a dinner knife. The sun made such a glory on the water, it seemed as if part of the glory overflowed into the dandelions on the ditch bank. I threw back my hair and laughed aloud.

"How beautiful!" I caroled and began to run down a narrow path toward the stream.

Bright red boulders walled the decline. After a few moments, the path turned a corner and I found myself staring at a maroon and gray knoll . . . shaped and fluted like a Christmas bell, each fluting edged in white.

My heart swelled. My throat ached. Even my fingertips tingled.

"Such grandeur," I whispered.

I felt awed, worshipful. I didn't move. The beauty was so splendid I was afraid it might be shattered by a breath.

Then, with a swish and a hop, a jackrabbit sat up in front of me. I jumped with surprise and the mood broke into bits.

The jackrabbit blinked at me uncertainly. After studying me, he decided I was harmless and settled on a grass sod where he lapped the warm golden sunshine as if it were honey.

I followed the path toward the stream. It turned again into a long brush-enclosed aisle. The shadows swallowed the slanting shafts of sunlight and my song returned.

Another climbing corner and there it was.

My melody halted at the sight: sky, sun, stretching brush, and the stream bursting into a thousand pieces of light whirling all about me. The red precipice on the other side flung itself downward in careless, stony abandon.

I stepped closer and took a deep breath.

The fragrance was damp and fresh, sweet and green.

The grass hugged the stream while the aspens chattered their leaves in welcome.

The aura of bloom was on everything. Flowers peeking out of the tall grasses called "Joy!" Their exuberant freshness, their bursting bloom . . . expanding, opening up, spilling over with anticipation seemed to beckon: HERE IS LIFE, BEAUTY, WONDER.

Did they beckon me, I wondered.

Specifically me?

Of course not! I grinned at my wistfulness.

And yet . . . I was included.

For their call was universal.

Steeped in splendor . . .

I could see, hear, feel,
in God's world of nature,

the clear invitation to life's finest and best. My heart responded . . . and reached for a dream!

This is merely an example of the activity involved in becoming "Expert in Home-cosmography"; this is a sample of the work involved in tilling your "inner land."

You observe. You listen. You experience. You *know*.

You record. You assimilate. You write.

From such tilling, your land may yield the marvelous essays, poetry, and fiction that are uniquely *your own* harvest.

Did you note in my "exercise" the rules we've discussed in use? This is a piece written solely as a part of my personal record of living with no retouching . . . yet the fundamentals of "putting words together" effectively can become so much a part of one's expression, they are an ever-ready part of communication.

This is your goal.

You can achieve it by developing deliberately your own "inner land."

Know! Record. Assimilate. Write.

14

THE CHALLENGE

Your Journal and your Notebook are your best friends.
Cultivate them.
John Cheever said:

When I began to write I found that this was the best way *to make sense of my life.* Literature is indescribably useful, or can be, simply as a passion or in finding a meaning or identity. What I like to call the youthfulness of the spirit will never die. . . .

I can't say as I'm ever at a lack for a stimulation to write. An author must be sensitive to everything around him to allow him to record his impressions as accurately as possible . . . he lives at a very thin-skinned level.

From "A Talk with John Cheever"
by Richard Poziak in *Prospectus*

When you become "Expert in Home-
cosmography" . . . when you are
"sensitive to everything around
[you] to allow [you] to record
[your] impressions as accurately

as possible" . . .
you will be able to write creatively
for yourself
                for your God
                            for others!

15

THE WRITING OF
LETTERS

Perhaps the most uniquely meaningful and yet the most over-looked form of writing creatively is the personal letter. Written to a reader who is interested in every detail simply *because* of the by-line, the letter is the most wondrous of all written-communication forms.

Letters may be written in all styles for all reasons and on all occasions. I would like for us to consider a few specifics.

The Everyday . . .

There may be those in your life with whom you correspond on a regular basis. When I was in college, I wrote my parents once a week. Years later, when they had to enter a rest home and their lives were more lonely, I made it a point to write to them every day. I even mailed a letter to my father on Friday morning before rushing to his town that evening to discover his death. On Monday, the day of his funeral, he received a letter from me!

My brother, Joe, took the letter and poised it on his fingers. He looked at me tenderly and said: "Great was her faithfulness."

I still have that letter . . . still unopened. It is a symbol of one of my best gifts to my parents. In those last years when illness forced inactivity, they could look forward to one touch from me every day.

Many look at me almost in disbelief when I say I wrote every day to my loved ones. They believe it an impossibility on the hectic schedule I kept in my professional and personal life. But letters can be written at midnight; on the handles of grocery carts when standing in line; on the seat of the car when waiting at a red light; on lecterns before delivering a college lecture; and even on the back of a book as one walks from one building to another!

This is true because a letter need not be formal, ponderous, or long. They can be joyfully debonair, even silly, and brief. Since my mother (and after her death, my father) saved all of my letters, I chose one to keep. It is an example of the latter style:

WE!
WHEE!
How I Thank God
We Are Three!

It was signed, Love, Ruth.

That was the entire letter. But I am sure it brought tears of love and chuckles of laughter from them both. I imagine they read it numerous times before it found its way to the letter box. And it probably took me all of sixty seconds to write those nine words, stuff them in an envelope and leave it on my mailbox.

(Perhaps I should explain that letter. My parents had eight children. They "concluded" their family with seven. Nine years after that "conclusion" came the stunning realization that another was on the way. I was *that* one!!! The "concluding" son left for college when I was eight and so I grew up, virtually, as an only child. So, except for holiday forays of siblings, it was the "three of us" during all my growing-up years. And a more loving trio was never formed!)

Regular correspondents (whether they be weekly or daily, monthly or annually) offer a unique channel for thinking, feeling, and sharing. The first reason for that is their *caring* about whatever you share . . . because you are you. Another is the versatility possible when writing in all of life's moods. One can ream out a recording of life's events, the emotional response, the intellectual response . . . which is all heart-sharing with another . . . one of life's *best* joys. The third important attribute of regular letter writing is the feedback to your activities, your feelings, your emerging philosophies . . . and your communication of them. You can know, from returned letters, how clear was your expres-

sion, how vivid was your sharing *and* how logical it might all
seem to one not subjectively immersed in the events.

If you do not have this habit now, I invite you to consider establishing it with at least one or two important people in your
world. It will augment your Journal work because it *will* be sharing and has feedback. It will augment your Notebook work because you can attempt to use the best means of expression. It will
give invaluable practice in the skill of writing for a reader. *And* it
will give you another record of WHO YOU ARE, WHY YOU
ARE. And that is important.

The only way, however, it will give you a permanent record is
if you ask those important people to preserve your letters. You'll
be amazed at how glad they are to establish a "letter box" and,
five years from now, you will find a unique record of your experiences of the "now" . . . unique from the Journal because you
were writing for eyes other than your own . . . unique from the
Notebook because you aren't polishing phrases, but the polishing
is ever ongoing as the rules, principles, et cetera, become inherent
in your language.

Now.

I have made that invitation totally for what it will do for *you*.
There is another consideration.

The gift your regular letters are to the recipient.

Every parent I have ever known (regardless of the exterior
relationship) is overjoyed to receive any kind of communiqué
from their child. Because I was a small child at home with parents who rejoiced with such excitement over every letter that
came from grown offspring, I am probably especially certain of
this fact. No matter how bleak life might be for my parents, one
brief note from one child could turn the sun on. I remember, during the Korean War, my mother was very ill. She could hardly
move any part of her body. Finances were strained. The whole
world pivoted in greenery-yallery mist.

One noontime, I was home from school when the mail came.
Among the bills was a letter from Korea. Immediately the shadows of our lives began to recede.

With shaking hands, my father opened the letter. My brother,
who was in combat, scrawled that he was writing on his helmet in
a foxhole . . . but he wanted to say, even then, even there, that

he loved his parents. The tears, unchecked, streamed down my father's cheeks and my mother sobbed into her pillow. I was fifteen and I took the precious note, . . . heavy with love . . . and kissed it.

My mother was still ill. Finances were still limited. Life was still less-than-ideal. But . . . because of a hastily scrawled note . . . all those things slipped into the background as our hearts bulged with gratitude for the love of a young soldier . . . and his writing to *tell us so!*

There is no greater gift a child can give a parent (I know from observation!) than regular writing of letters.

There is no greater gift a parent can give a child (I know from personal experience!) than regular writing of letters.

There is no greater gift one can give any family member, lover, or friend than regular sharing in a steady stream of love letters . . . for in that stream, the recipient always has a love glow!

Letters on Special Days . . .

My grandparents did it for my mother . . .

My mother did it for her children . . .

I, now, do it for my children . . .

Perhaps, one day, they shall do it for their own. . . . The gift of writing special letters on special days.

Every birthday brought a letter:

I leaf through some of them and smile. Here's one on a very yellowed sheet. It begins: "December 30 . . . Fifty years ago you were placed in my arms as a baby . . . how wonderful you were!" That was written to my mother by her mother. And now I hold that fragile paper on which love was written thirty-eight years ago. It details memories of a day which occurred eighty-eight years ago. How I cherish it.

That birthday letter was important to my mother when she received it at age fifty. It is important to me as, with misty eyes, I peruse the love relationship between that mother and daughter thirty-eight years later. It may be important to my grandchild who, in the year 2000, ponders upon the constancy of love.

Here is one written to me:

> "Happy eighth birthday, little girl! You have a bad bruise on your leg from falling out of a tree. Sometimes I despair your ever being a lady . . . but as I watch you sleeping this

morning, your hair clinging to the pillow like melted fudge, your lashes long on pink cheeks, I know that femininity is there. Oh my little eight-year-old, one day you *will* be a lady!"

The tears come.

I dare not read farther.

The "little eight-year-old" did become a lady who wore high heels, furs, and overwhelmed her mother with feminine charms, but the warm encircling love of that mother for her eight-year-old tomboy was *the* vital constant in life. That letter is priceless. I leaf through more letters in the "birthday box" and find my letters to Billy, age twelve, to Ron, age five. Here is a recent message. My heart glows warm. It was written by my son: "Happy Birthday Moddy! [his pet name for me] This is the day for me to tell you (again) that you are the greatest of all mothers, but I want to tell you something else too. You are my best, my very best, friend. . . ."

Again tears come.

Quickly I have sheafed through four generations of love expressed on birthdays . . . making happy the present moment . . . preserving it for all time. What wonder. Love made permanent . . . glowing memories of a birth to be shared . . . eighty-eight years AFTER THE FACT!

Anniversaries always bring special letters.

I can hardly read the letter I wrote Bill on our first wedding anniversary. We were very poor (in worldly goods) so my typewriter ribbon was soooo dim. But as I squint at the dimming words, I read:

"My darling, One whole wonderful year has gone since the night I walked down the aisle and became Mrs. Bill Vaughn. How little we knew then of the future that lay before us: the ecstatic happiness, the sorrows, the tears . . . but through everything the majestic heartbeat of love. Oh this wonderful year! I want it engraved forever on our hearts! I want to hold it close to me now and remember every moment of it . . . the precious moments of love . . . the glorious moments of laughter . . . the maturing moments of tears and pain . . . the thrilling moments of high adventure . . . the hallowed moments of togetherness . . ."

A quarter of a century has passed. I still feel the same way.

About every year. How grateful I am for this letter that details, in pages, those specific moments of that specific year.

I gave this letter to Bill as we prepared for bed that night. I remember his sitting there reading it. When he finished, he had tears in his eyes as he opened wide his arms to thank me. It was important then.

It is important now.

Perhaps it shall be important to our children or their children in years to come. A record of love-beyond-understanding.

Thanksgiving Day should always bring special letters.

Isn't that what Thanksgiving Day is all about: expressing THANKSGIVING . . . to God . . . to those who bring us joy.

I have a special Journal in which, once a year, I have written a poem beginning with the same words:

> Because it is Thanksgiving Day
> I'll pause . . . and softly I shall pray.
> I'll thank my God. . . .

And from that point on, each poem is different because each year brings different specifics for which I want to give my THANKSGIVING to God! Whenever I am whammed with self-pity and feel, of all people, the most slighted, I go to that Journal and, within a few pages, my heart is almost splitting with gratitude for all the specific blessings enumerated therein.

My husband is usually one of the world's least expressive people. It is our family joke that I write reams of pages to him and he signs a card: "I love you very much!" But even before our marriage, he began striving for expression. Every special day of our life together has brought his letter. Plus many unexpected. In fact, at times, he overwhelms me with his expressiveness.

A recent Thanksgiving brought this letter he had written in a motel room the week prior. He had been attending a seminar where one of the lecturers was an extremist in the women's lib movement. That night he wrote one of the longest letters of his life. I will share just a part.

"This is my annual letter where I share with you my prayer of thanksgiving to God that you are mine. This year it will be a bit different. I have heard for the last several hours the thesis that women are no different from men. I sit here, look at your picture, and thank God that is not true.

"I ponder on the gifts you give to me BECAUSE YOU ARE UNIQUELY WOMAN. These are some of the things that come quickly to mind.

"You are my love. Not only is your body uniquely my love, but the soft, tender, giving spirit that prompts your caresses and kisses is my love. In that feminine charm, you delight me in every quest for love.

" 'You turn the world on with your smile.' I know that's a line from Mary Tyler Moore's theme song but it is one I often hum when I think of you. Your warm smile in that small womanly face is the focus for making my whole world . . . not only go round . . . but make sense. It is a woman's gentle, understanding, joyful smile that 'turns on my world.' I live with the texture of men; what I need most from you is the special glow of femininity.

" 'You Light Up My Life!' is Debby Boone's song. But, again, it runs through my head day after day as I thank God for you. . . ."

Is there a doubt in your mind that a million dollars could not buy *that* letter? It is lengthy . . . but I can recite it word for word . . . and often do . . . in the midnight of pain when I lie humanly alone . . . but magnificently bundled in this coverlet of Bill's love.

No greater gift than a letter!

Ever!

Christmas

Valentine's Day

First Day of Summer

On *any* day that is uniquely special in your life, in your relationship with another.

My illness has stimulated a barrage of letters in my marriage. Because of my having to change from hyperactivity to a "little old lady," my ego has been severely battered. My wise husband has kept me flooded with cards, notes, letters assuring me of his love. I, in turn, have tried to share the agonies of a life-gone-crazy in letters to him . . . since to try to talk about it makes me cry! As I peruse this collection, I find an astonishing portrait of the ideal of marriage.

Here is a letter I wrote on an "ordinary day":

"Dearest Bill, I wish I could be perfect for you! You never asked me to be, but I would like to give you such a gift because I love you so.

"You give me the gift of perfection these days. You make me feel wanted in spite of my swollen face and body. You listen to me when the torrents of frustration seem ready to overflow all boundaries. You quietly accept and understand this illness with all its implications, all its complications as FACT and look at life from THAT vantage point. You hold me steady when all my life-long philosophies and concepts are shattering about me. And I thank you. There is nothing else I can do. I wish I could. I wish I could be perfect for you. But since that is a gift I cannot give, I want you to know how gratefully I receive your gift of not ASKING for perfection . . . but ACCEPTING me as I am. . . ."

Our relationship is stronger because of our written communiqués. It is preserved for our children to ponder. In a world where marriages crumple at the slightest provocation, here is written evidence of a marriage that never wavered when caught in the hurricane of life-changing illness.

We love each other more *in* the writing.

We cherish the record personally. Others may find the record inspiring . . . even stabilizing.

There may be times
When you want
To write
A series of letters
For a special occasion.

Consider.

One of my favorite books to give to bridal couples is one called *Letters to Karen* written by Charlie Shedd. He said that his daughter, Karen, asked him how she could have as good a marriage as her parents. He tried to tell her in these letters written as a wedding gift for her.

I have done this for many of my special friends. I shall do this for each of my sons, God willing. Not for publication, as were Charlie Shedd's . . . but for personal love-giving.

I write of the uniqueness of the love, union, married future of the couple. I share my own thoughts, feelings, philosophies, "keys" to success . . . and then I take these to a bindery, have them bound in white leather, and stamped with a title in gold with my by-line. It is my most personal love gift. And, often, the most cherished wedding gift that can be received.

One of my friends is a minister. He has been writing letters to his son since the child's birth. In them, he details his changing perceptions, his evolving philosophies about birth, life, death, God. . . .

His son is now in seminary . . . He will graduate this spring. His graduation gift will be this bound collection of his father's letters. As this young man enters the ministry, can you imagine a gift that could rival this one in importance? Discussion of sermons that were good. Discussion of sermons that were bad. Discussion of theology that was good. Discussion of theology that was bad. Discussion written in the dynamics of life . . . now to be available for his son's perusal through all of his life . . . and for generations to come.

One day a friend and I were enjoying her inimitable cherry pie with her teenage daughter. As Debbie finished, she said: "Mom, how *do* you make crust like that? I've never eaten crust anywhere that compares with yours."

Carol immediately began the details of how she mixed ingredients, but Debbie was whirling away into her own world. We blinked at each other. . . . It was such a *good* question, but she didn't wait for the answer . . . and one day she'd need to know . . . Ah!

We both got the idea at the same time!

"I'll write it to her!" Carol said.

So immediately we began to plan "Letters to Debbie on . . .
How to make piecrust
How to make biscuits that rise
How to fry eggs that won't stick. . . ."

At sixteen, Debbie had the perception to ask the question. But her attention span was limited. She didn't *need* to know about piecrusts for years yet. But one day . . .

Carol went to work on her "Letters to Debbie . . ."

After I got home, I went to my mother's recipe book and looked at the notes written in the margins of its pages . . . the recipes jotted down amid all the flour and milk marks that warped the entire book. I was grateful for each.

I smiled at this one:

CORNBREAD   handful of flour
               handful of meal
               pinch of salt
               dash of soda; baking powder
               two eggs
               milk.

I am sure Betty Crocker would flinch at the precision of *that* recipe. But it had certainly created a stream of luscious pans of cornbread for my mother's lifetime.

I don't have a daughter to write a recipe book for. But I shall, someday, have daughters-in-law. They'll hear all about "Mama's Chocolate Pie" (Bill's grandmother); "Grandmommy's Grasshopper Pie" (Bill's mother); and "Moddy's German Chocolate Pie" (I really *am* a whiz at this!) . . . so wouldn't they like to know how to make all these dishes beloved by their husbands? I took plastic photo trays which are designed to stack on top of each other. Each contains dozens of plastic holders (for photos). In each holder, I have placed a favorite recipe. On the back side, I have written its history, e.g. Mama made a "Red Velvet Cake" for every Valentine's Day; on every summer visit; and left one frozen in the deep freeze. Both boys took pieces annually to their teachers because of the novelty of color and texture of the cake.

Sometimes the history is lengthy. The "letter" is longer than can be seen in the flap . . . thus it is neatly folded so that it can be taken out for reading . . . but succinctly sets forth initial facts at the first glimpse.

This particular set of trays (available in gift shops) has a top on which is a heavy gold monogram of the boy's initial. My future daughter-in-law (whoever she may be!) will have only to take out the tray containing the recipe desired, set it on a small stand (those which hold china plates, pictures, and so on), place a clothespin (enclosed with the package) on the recipe desired, and

there it is beside her mixing place with all directions. Whenever she desires to share the "history" of that dish, it is all
recorded in the back of the flap. And the plastic keeps it grease-
safe.

I grin to think of an unknown girl someday telling an unknown
child that "Grandmommy Vaughn first made this dish in their
first pastorate when they didn't have much money . . . and so she
became a genius with hamburger!" *I* will be that Grandmommy!
Oh boy! But . . . in this kind of sharing . . . it *could* be that one
day the unknown child would grow up to tell *her* child about
"Great-grandmommy Vaughn" who became a genius at hamburger dishes!!

What fun . . . to share with future generations . . . wisdom
learned in baking things. Carol's wonderful way with piecrust
. . . to my "Hamburger Stroganoff" created out of this, that, and
a pinch of paprika . . . in a moment of necessity!

A series of letters are tremendous to begin writing for any special occasion now, or in the future. I mentioned the letters written
by my minister friend for his son's seminary graduation. This
year, I had the joyful impetus of a contract for a book "for gradu-
ates" . . . and my son, Ron, was a high school senior.

I wrote that book for him.

And when I mailed the polished manuscript to the publisher, I
gave a longer, more personalized version, to my son. In it I had
tried to articulate the philosophies I felt would hold him steady as
he stepped from childhood into maturity.

The published book is a joy as I can share with the many.

The longer, personal book is the one *most cherished* by the
young man who *really* counts in my world. His response to it is
the one I cherish most.

I suppose the most important series of letters that I have un-
dertaken was a few years ago when this illness began. Because of
the rarity of the problem, a diagnosis was long in coming. March-
ing in and out of doctors' offices, plummeting in and out of hospitals, dragging in and out of test laboratories for two whole
years . . . I became ever weaker, ever more silent, ever nearer
Death . . . and I knew—

I didn't talk about it with anyone. Not even my doctor.

But I, deep inside, knew.

Life was draining away.

I looked at my two sons and thought my heart would burst from my body. They were so young . . . so vulnerable. . . . There were so many things I wanted to tell them. . . . And one day . . . I decided to do just that.

I began a series of letters to my sons in which I tried to set forth the residuum of wisdom I felt I had gained to that point in my life. I tried to write out the clues to life with God that I had gained. I tried to articulate the way I wanted them to feel about birth, life, death. I set down my own thoughts, feelings, faith. I assured them of my love, in this world, in any other world, for love is ongoing forever. Nothing, not even death, can change LOVE.

Finally it was decided I should be sent to a diagnostic hospital. Weary from the two-year journey downward, I was certain the elusive diagnosis would not be made; I would never return to my home.

So, without a word to anyone, I took my full collection of letters for my sons and placed them in my lockbox along with my last will and testament. I knew that when Bill found them, he would understand and know when to give them to my sons.

The diagnosis was made. Replacement therapy was instituted. I remained in my sons' lives . . . with gratitude and joy.

But the letters are still theirs.

They have, in black and white, the articulated statement of their mother's philosophy of life and love. . . . They have the tangible record of their mother's statement of faith in God and in immortality.

Whenever death separates us, they shall have, for their lifetime, that collection of letters deliberately written in deepest love to help them face life, to help them face death. That collection of letters is my finest gift to them.

There is one other "form" of letter writing I would like to explicitly mention. I alluded to it in my discussion of "Thanksgiving letters," but I want to specifically invite you to "Writing Letters to God."

I have found this to be one of the most meaningful forms of my communication with the Divine. In A. W. Tozer's book, *The*

Pursuit of God, he states that "communication is intercession between the created personality and the creating personality." I like that. As Creating Personality, God knows more about me than I know myself, . . . and I can approach Him in a love letter, as I can no other personality. He understands fully, deeply, completely. . . . And the knowledge of *that kind* of love makes letter writing to Him a wonderfully unique experience.

Whenever I feel deeply, I go to the typewriter for my prayer time. It is now a thoroughly ingrained habit.

> I pour out details
> I exhort "what should be"
> I lament "what is"
> I exult in "what is"
> I accept "what is"
> I laugh
> I cry
> I whimper and moan
> I pirouette and dance
> I pray
> I praise
> I worship
> I communicate . . .
>
> > with my God
> > in all my moods
> > in all life's seasons.

This is my best means of God-communication . . . in the *need* of sharing receiving from Him in the dynamic ongoingness of life. *And* it is a record forevermore of one human heart dialoguing with her God. I do invite you to the wonderful world of letter writing at all times to all your important people and to your God.

16

THE WRITING WITH PHOTOS

There is a professional published arena called "photo writing." You can find its fruits in magazines, in books, in slide presentations, and other places. I invite you to prepare for that arena by developing the skill in creations *important* to you and those close to you. When you are facile in the skill, if you care to, you may enter the professional published world. It utilizes the same principles here set down.

"Photo writing" may be defined as that communication which compresses the meaning of all the words into a visual picture, or articulates the myriad of meanings of a visual picture into words. It is, simply, combining two tools of expression so that one augments the other; one is not quite complete without the other.

If the form is unfamiliar to you, I suggest you peruse some bookstores. The Walter Rinder books, published by Celestial Arts, are good examples. Gloria Gaither's *Make Warm Noises,* published by Impact, is good. The Charles Swindoll books published by Multnomah are exemplary.

I began my own form of "photo writing" in the summer before I married Bill. I was feeling such a myriad of exploding, bewildering, and skyrocketing emotions that I found words insufficient. Because I knew nothing of photography, I went to my huge collection of magazines. I spent hours searching for the *right* picture to "compress the meaning of all the words" I wrote into a

THE WRITING WITH PHOTOS

visual picture. Occasionally I found a picture that sent me scurrying to the typewriter to "articulate the myriad of meanings" of the visual picture into words of my world.

I put all of that effort into a scrapbook that I gave Bill as a wedding gift. He was so delighted with it that I kept at it through the years.

I pulled out an old red scrapbook. It is the one which contains the photo-writing account of our first pastorate. On the first page, I have typed this poem:

Between the covers of this book
We keep the golden past . . .
When we entered our first parsonage
And a parish was ours . . . at last . . .
And every season each in turn
That saw us laugh and play . . .
And solve our problems with our love
And grow happier day by day . . .
The pictures of our dreams-come-true;
The ecstacy we shared . . .
The million little things we did
To show how much we cared . . .
The pranks and stunts and laughter
The joy of being one . . .
The record of our unfolding love . . .
Through tears and smiles and fun . . .
And as the years go rolling by . . .
I only hope that we . . .
Compile a dozen other books . . .
As dear to you and me.

And we have.
In all the varied changing of life's seasons for us.

I invite you to the creative task of photo writing in your world. You can record life with words and movies, words and art, words and sketches, but I shall present chiefly the combination of words and photos or words and slides.

Words and slides offer a totally different dimension . . . because you can add sound.

It is an exciting world.

If you are interested, but uninformed about such things as projector dissolves and triple projectors showing triple montages of
visual images, et cetera, go to a camera shop and ask to *be* informed. An alert salesman will be glad to show you all the mar-
vels of the slide cameras, projectors, and give you brochures and
booklets detailing the creative ways such can be used.

Your mind will go a million directions with the ways you can
work slides, words, sound effects, music, and other effects in your
expression. I doubt any other medium holds quite *this* degree of
freedom of communication.

I have used this medium professionally for the Church Mis-
sions Department, the Church Schools Department, The Cancer
Foundation, et cetera. But again, the creations most meaningful
to me are those created about and for my personal world.

I believe that will be true for you. So . . . Welcome!

That word leads nicely to my most ambitious project of combining slides and words. Bill became my photographer for all this
and he *is* prolific. He is most disconcerting because he is apt to
take a picture *anywhere, anytime!*

From that plethora of slides, I have culled those to make a
many-canistered, ever-ongoing slide presentation. It begins in
our first pastorate and continues through today. When I first set it
up, I put slides in a permanent arrangement in carousels. They
are never disturbed. When we want to share the story of our lives
with someone . . . or, especially at Christmas, we want to "trek
down memory's lane," we simply set up the projector and let one
carousel follow another through all the years.

I made a tape with musical background and chosen sound
effects that can be played simultaneously. As each slide is flashed
on the screen, the music and my words record the story of life in
the Bill Vaughn household through all the orbiting seasons of
marriage, pastorates, small boys, graduate school, growing boys,
college professors, grown boys to now . . . and it is all entitled:
Welcome to Our World!

Everytime there is a new carousel of pictures completed, I add
to the tape, trying to keep it current, ongoing as a photo-writing
record, which is a visual audible *experience.*

Photo writing (with slides) is used in this way for personal historical records. But this unique medium may be used beautifully for gifts.

When the children were small, I used to write a script which was set up in the professional way like this:

AUDIO	VIDEO
Here I wrote the words plus music or sound effects. The page is divided into two distinct columns. You may buy paper with set margins for you. You may simply set your own as I have done here.	Here I described the picture I needed to "compress the meaning of my words" into a visual image.

When the pictures were ready, I made the tape (complete with music and sound effects) and mailed it with a carousel to doting grandparents or proud uncles so they could "share" in the growing days of two *very special* little boys. Can you imagine a better "Mother's Day" gift for a grandmother?

On one occasion, an artistic friend drew cartoons of which we took slides to visually illustrate a script I wrote on *The Hazards of Graduate School*. It was a class project and received rave reviews! Fun creation. Treasured visual/audible record.

For one of the boy's birthday celebrations, Bill photographed crazy antics of our friends, our dogs, and ourselves in slides visualizing the script of a story I wrote called: "The Red Baron's Mystery." (We had two Irish setters; the male was named The Red Baron!) That carousel of slides was "set" to a tape of a kaleidoscope of syncopated music that made little boys (*and* their dignified parents!) scream with laughter . . .

A script setting up visual and audible effects must be written for slides. Although I have preserved most of my creations on tape, the script may also be read live with live background. This is effective and may be desirable for certain communications. The complete script may be filed with the carousels, thus always available for use when needed.

For writing with photos, scripts are unnecessary. The pictures will grow out of your words on the page . . . or the other way around . . . but they form a unit within themselves. Nothing else, such as sound, will be added. This is creativity for the eye alone.

As I mentioned in the beginning, I began photo writing with magazine pictures because those were the only illustrative materials available. For my personal photo writing, I still use these.

I have already shared the time when Bill was critically ill. I wrote my "compressed emotions" in poetry through all those long anxious days and nights.

At his return to my world, I typed all these, pasted them on pages of construction paper, illustrated them with selected magazine pictures, and had them bound into a book as a love gift for my returned-Bill. The magazine pictures add a dimension that could not have been achieved by the words alone. If real photos are not available, I recommend your consideration of this means of illustration. One of my friends paid fifteen dollars for a book whose photographs seemed uniquely fitting for a gift she was making for her fiancé's wedding gift. When I perused the finished product, I knew it was well worth the money!

When possible, of course, photos taken from real life are best. Included in this kind of writing, one also should use "real" memorabilia to enhance the recording of an event, a feeling, a life season.

When Billy was born, I set aside a box in which I kept all my letters to him, thoughts about him, prayers to God for him . . . my poetry . . . my essays . . . my philosophies . . . *AND* all the photos and memorabilia that accompanied his growth. When Ron was born, I began an identical box. I tried to keep both faithfully through the years.

When Billy was in his senior year in high school, I got out his box and went all through it. I organized it from birth to the moment of his graduation, and then I typed it in a formal book of photo writing where is set down the recorded mother/son relationship from birth to end of high school where I "release" him as a young man. In it I try to detail our shared encounters with life. And God. And reaching. And growth. And change. And LOVE that remains!

At our family graduation party, Billy opened this last box. In it, he found the book, bound in red leather, entitled:

BILLY EDWARD VAUGHN, JR.
Produced by Bill and Ruth Vaughn

He began to read it aloud to the assembled family. And as the pages were turned, his voice grew shakier and shakier until, finally, the young Stoic burst into tears.

The entire family was crying.

I took the book and continued with the reading. And my seventeen-year-old football player listened, wept unashamedly, laughed delightedly, and understood the inestimable personal VALUE of himself in his parents' world.

When Ron graduated from high school this year, he received his red-leather-bound book entitled

RONALD CHARLES VAUGHN
Produced by Bill and Ruth Vaughn

with the same joy and sense of cherishing as did Billy.

Each book concludes:

> Tall young stranger
> On the move
> Child I used to know . . .
> Go . . .
> > Where you will . . .
> Here is your
> "Come-back" key:

"I'LL ALWAYS LOVE YOU!"

Photo writing is one of the most beautiful forms of writing creatively. It may be done for an entire life segment (like the boys' books); it may be done for a special period (such as Bill's illness); it may be done for an event you would like to celebrate.

When Bill earned his Ph.D., I wrote a manuscript of photo writing recording the decision to leave the full-time pastorate to return to graduate school with two little boys in tow . . . all the way through the earning of the M.Div. degree in seminary, the M.A. degree at KU; and now the ultimate Ph.D. at KU. It took ten years for all of that to transpire and so I entitled the book: *Decade of Daring*. It is his most-prized graduation gift.

For any event: birthday, Christmas, or Valentine's, or just for sharing's sake . . . photo writing can be one of your most beautifully eloquent, most clearly expressive, most deeply meaningful forms of creative sharing!

17

THE WRITING OF
MEDITATIONS

In college, it is called "exposition" which quite literally means to set forth a subject . . . appeal to the understanding . . . challenge comprehension. Professionally, you will find it in magazine articles, newspaper editorials, and essays that range in style from Erma Bombeck to William F. Buckley, Jr.

It seems simpler, more self-explanatory, to call this most common form of writing "meditations." The definition I have evolved and prefer is: a person thinking, evaluating, interpreting life.

Whatever the term used, this is one of the most useful forms of expression and communication. This is your major prose style for your writing in letters, in photo writing, and in all other manuscripts where your goal is thinking, evaluating, interpreting life.

So. Let's consider the "how to" principles of such writing.

There are six fundamentals of a good creative meditation. We will discuss each in depth, but briefly they are: (1) a provocative idea; (2) a strong title; (3) an intriguing beginning; (4) an appropriate structure; (5) effective anecdotes; (6) a forceful conclusion.

1. A Provocative Idea.

"Life is a petty thing," says Ortega, "unless it is moved by the indomitable urge to extend its boundaries. Only in proportion as we are desirous of living more do we really live." The creative process is more an exploration and a profound learning than it is the tangible result. Mark Van Doren wrote that man is "a nervous animal, straining to comprehend what he contains, straining even to contain it." The writer must be a thinker, a philosopher, a grappler of ideas. Exposition—Meditation—demands that you lift the sail, catch the winds of life wherever they drive your boat . . . open yourself to explore the full emotions and experiences of life well-lived.

Narration tells a story. Description paints a picture. Dialogue records conversation. Argument states a case. . . . But Exposition—Meditation—is, in my view, that incomparable exhilaration of "thinking, evaluating, interpreting life" as it appears in your *own* experience.

To that exhilaration, I invite you in this chapter.

Interested?

If so, your first question probably is: *Where* do the provocative ideas come from?

Myriads of sources.

Here are a few.

A. *Your Journal.*
B. *Your Notebook.*
C. *Your Reading.*

Lucille Vaughan Payne, in her book *The Lively Art of Writing,* talks very effectively about the "informed opinion." This is what the writer obtains in exploring the philosophies and concepts of diverse personalities as revealed in their writing. The writer of exposition, meditations, *must* be a reader. From this habit comes general information, specific information, theories, and problems . . . provocative *ideas*.

My cousin, who is a Ph.D., works for the Educational Research Council of America. He made a "Personal List of Impact Paperbacks" that he felt all teachers, special school personnel, and administrators should read. I think it is excellent for all who *think* and are concerned with issues. Perhaps this list of books will stimulate your own search.

AUTHOR	TITLE	PUBLISHER
Viktor Frankl	*Man's Search for Meaning*	Washington Square Press

Divided into two parts—Frankl's true experiences in Nazi concentration camps, with the second part dealing with the basic concepts of "logotherapy"—this book shows the importance of each individual's discovering meaning and purpose in his life.

| Erich Fromm | *Man for Himself* | Fawcett Publications |

Highlights of this book include Fromm's distinction between "Rational" and "Irrational" authority; Fromm's discourse on "Self-Love" as being essential to the love of any other self; and his discussion on "Rational" and "Irrational" faith.

| Arthur Jersild | *In Search of Self* | Teachers College Press Columbia University |

This book deals with self-understanding.

| David Wilkerson | *The Cross and the Switchblade* | Pyramid N–2189 |

True story of rehabilitated youth who were hooked on hate and drugs.

| Nicky Cruz | *Run Baby Run* | Logos Books |

Tough gang leader gives testimonial of how he responded to love and trust.

| Bill Sands | *My Shadow Ran Fast* | Signet T 3939 |

A man tells of discovering meaning to life while vainly wishing for death in solitary confinement in San Quentin.

| E. R. Braithwaite | *To Sir with Love* | Pyramid X–1608 |

True story of the impact of a teacher on teenage rebellion.

| Margaret Landon | *Anna and the King of Siam* | Pocket Books |

Novel based on the true life experiences of Anna Leonowens who made a major impact on the entire Court of Siam.

From *Annotated Bibliography*
J. Wright Griggs, Ph.D.

C. S. Lewis   *The Problem of Pain*   Macmillan
The Introduction alone is vital to stimulating thought that will lead to sound personal philosophy.

Bertrand Russell   *Why I Am Not a*   Simon & Schuster
                      Christian
The text of a speech, this provides argument that challenges mind-stretching logic of its reader.

Charles Colson   *Born Again*   Chosen Books
The account of a man's confrontation with the Divine and the results that changed the lives of thousands.

This kind of list could go on indefinitely. For you, in your Notebook and mental processes, it should. You cannot present an "informed opinion" until you have reasoned issues with other people from other backgrounds with other points of view.

One of the stimulations for ideas can come in the diversity of your reading itself. One of my favorite pieces came from a "provocative idea" gained in comparing the two philosophies of marriage as stated by Peter Marshall in *A Man Called Peter* . . . and by Jane Fonda in an interview in *Redbook*. Marshall, in an excerpt from one of his sermons, states that "The average woman, if she gives her full time to her home, her husband, her children . . . will be engaged in a life work that will demand every ounce of her strength, every bit of her patience, every talent God has given her, the utmost sacrifice of her love . . . And she will find that for which she was created. She will know that she is carrying out the plan of God." In contrast, Fonda stated: "I always felt instinctively that there is something wrong in the idea of two people living together because of a signature on a paper, or in the idea of a woman swearing to love and to cherish and to obey. . . . Do you know why marriage can be wrong? Because the normal process of a human being is to change, and marriage prevents people from changing. . . . The family structure is the result of a [polit-ical] system, that makes women . . . a class of slaves."

From exploring these two poles of thought, my own mind was challenged to sort it through and strive to articulate my personal philosophy of marriage. From those two stimuli of reading came a provocative idea that gave me one of my most rewarding expe-riences of "thinking, evaluating, interpreting life."

Another stimulus of reading is the positing of problems you may not have dealt with mentally. Not only does this furnish "provocative ideas" for writing, but will provide a firm founda-tion for you when life slaps you with the same complexity.

I remember when I first read Catherine Marshall's *Christy*. I was enchanted with the young schoolteacher who went to the Ap-palachian Mountains to teach. There, she met a Quaker woman, Miss Alice, who was a tower of strength, a fountain of wisdom.

In chapter thirty-three, Miss Alice shares with Christy her per-sonal story. She had been raped as a teenager, bore a child, and all of her life plans were rearranged as a result.

My reaction was total protest.

I had learned to love Miss Alice in the book and my mind screamed: "If God is all-powerful, why does He allow such suffering? If God can do anything, why did He not protect the in-nocent, truth-seeking girl from the evil-scheming man? If God is love, why did the sin have to happen to Alice? Even so, why, then, did she have to bear the child? *Why* do sincere, pure, inno-cent people have to suffer?"

Springboarding from this dilemma came the broader one of the problem of pain in our world. I had never spent the time and effort to sort it all out in my mind until confronted with the prob-lem in my reading. Since that time, the question has searingly be-come my own. I am grateful for the beginnings of my thought processes stimulated years before I was personally involved.

Few of us take the pains to study the origin of our beliefs or the logic of them. It is easier to continue to believe what people tell us . . . the rosy clichés . . . the pious platitudes. But the writer should deliberately strive to *reason* through his convictions . . . and strive to avoid the trap of looking only for arguments that enforce a current position. Be open for diverse points of view. Never run away from questions.

A collegian called my home late one night. After the first pleasantries, he launched into a barrage of challenging interrogations that seemed almost endless. When he finished, he paused hesitantly and then said: "I suppose you think I'm a heretic!" I said: "I think you are an honestly seeking young man whom I admire. If religion is to be a vital force in your life, you must never be hesitant to question. Christianity is strong; it can stand the assault of probing questions; there are answers that will satisfy. But you have to be willing to search for them."

This is the challenge of the writing of exposition, of meditations. It demands the courageous honesty to "think, evaluate, interpret life" in as wide and thorough a dimension as you can. Reading will be one of your greatest assists.

D. *The Telephone Book.*

To broaden the horizons of my college students in gaining ideas for exposition, I took them on many field trips. Before a course began, I would sit with the phone book to look for unusual mind-stretching places to explore. I came up with many more each semester than we were able to visit as a class. Many of my students continued with the list I made available to them, and some striking pieces of writing came from ideas born in perusing a telephone book!

Here is a part of one list:

Jesus' Crash Pad . . . (a place where dope addicts could "crash" and receive physical, emotional, spiritual assistance)

Inspiration House . . . (place where people were available twenty-four hours a day for allowing visitors into a religious art gallery, record library with earphones, and library)

The Helping Hand . . . (homey setting where people were available twenty-four hours a day to sit down with coffee and talk over problems with anyone in need)

Our Saviour's Convent . . . (home where nuns live in constant prayer and are not allowed to speak except in certain places at certain times; they spoke with my students through a barrier)

The Old Cathedral . . . (an old Catholic church featuring beautiful hand-carved "Stations of the Cross")

In our fascinating world, there is a prolifera of ideas awaiting in arenas that are outside our regular daily routines. When you feel the courage to take on a "new world," get out the telephone book, make appointments at interesting-sounding places, and your mind will go wild with ideas.

E.   *The Reader's Guide to Periodical Literature.*

Available in any public library, you can find written materials catalogued on every subject imaginable.

F.   *The Newspaper Morgue.*

Every newspaper has a collection of its own published material, indexed by subject, which is loaded with information and ideas.

G.   *The Government Printing Office. Washington, D.C.*

This is the repository of the greatest accumulation of facts and figures in the world. And most of them are in pamphlet form, free for the asking. If there is a fee, it is slight. When you need additional ideas or material, write them of your problem. You'll be amazed at the dimension of their helpful resources.

H.   *Interviews.*

An hour with a fascinating personality can give you a year's worth of writing ideas. One of my students was so intrigued with the people at The Helping Hand that he interviewed several of the leaders. He came away with story ideas and illustrative material for meditations that would take a lifetime to develop. I remember so well his return from those interviews. He came to my office, flopped in a chair, and just shook his head. After quite a lengthy silence, he said: "Truth *is* stranger than fiction!"

I.   *Your personal files.*

One of the small niceties of life is that filing folders fit *exactly* in shoe boxes! Although when you are rich and famous, you will want a filing cabinet . . . at this point, shoe boxes will serve you well.

Purchase a supply of filing folders and place them upright in your shoe box. Write on their label tips the general topics in which you are interested. Be sure you have many empty ones because your horizon will expand rapidly.

Ask all your friends to give you their magazines when they are finished with them. Those gifts plus your own magazines and newspapers will form a reservoir of idea stimulators that is as rich as Fort Knox. Never allow a magazine or newspaper to be filed in one piece. When you are finished with it, go through and rip out everything that interests you . . . including pictures . . . and throw it in the file bearing a title of that general category. Be a saver . . . even of subjects that you think you would never write about. If you go to work for a magazine sometime, you never know what an editor will ask for. I have been given assignments on everything from beavers to General Motors!

When you feel an impulse to write about a specific subject (prayer, for example), go to that file and look through all the articles, columns, and pictures that you have been accumulating under that title. Your perusal of that material will begin to stimulate your own thoughts until you are "fired" for the best exposition, the best meditation on that topic possible.

Another helpful use of the files is that when you read a book that deals graphically with a topic in certain sections, write down the reference material and put it in that folder. You may have forgotten the book entirely when you sit down to write on the subject, but that reference notation will bring it flooding back.

2. A Strong Title.

When should you choose a title?

First, middle, or last?

The answer is: None of the above!

You choose a title when it occurs to you . . . and that may be the night before it goes to press . . . and it may be years before you ever write the first word! One of the lists you may want to keep in your Notebook is of intriguing titles that evolve in your life venture.

Be constantly on the alert for strong titles because this is the first thing that your reader will see . . . and, later when you think of publishing, it will be the first thing an editor will see . . . and that *is* important. An editor usually has a pile of manuscripts on his desk. He usually will thumb through them quickly . . . and the one with the most catchy title is the one read first . . . and with the greatest degree of receptivity.

You can find titles in phrases from your reading, from your listening, from your own perusing, from specific searching, and from moments of nitty-gritty living! Probably my best book title is *Lord, Keep the Ducks!* which is about life in our first pastorate. It came, literally, in a moment of total exasperation with the entire setup. I was twenty years old, trying to be the competent mistress of a parish with teeming activities and challenges. One day it all crushed in on me and I cried: "Next time, I'll try raising ducks, Lord! This parsonage is too much for me!"

Just at that moment, a knock came at the door (again!!!) . . . and when I dried my eyes, I invited in a small freckle-faced boy who shared with me an essay he had written for school telling about the "most important" things in his life which were God, his pastor, love . . . and the tears that filled my eyes, in that moment, were surging from gratitude. I whispered: "Lord, keep the ducks! I'll carry on with the parsonage for now . . . and thank You, God! Thank You from the depths of my heart!"

Later when I wrote that account, I remembered the true-life incident, and in that phrase came my title.

Another title I have always loved is *At Whatever Hour You Come*. It is a phrase I noted in a book written by Dr. Tom Dooley. Years later I wrote a book by that title and structured it on that concept. Because there were many books published at that time about the second coming, the book editor felt that the public might consider the title indicative of that subject and asked me to change it. I did to *Even When I Cry* . . . which, I think, has proven to be a strong title, but I have always loved the first one, which came out of a book.

There are three rules to selecting a title for your work.

(1)   Keep it short and crisp.
(2)   It must have relevance to the topic.
(3)   It must have some quality of music or surprise, curiosity or stimulation, or reader-recognition shock.

I think *Even When I Cry* has both the first and last characteristics of (3). It is musical in sound, and every person recognizes the life experience of the season of tears. *Lord, Keep the Ducks!* has the elements of surprise and curiosity stimulation. I've had all kinds of unexpected, laughable reactions to that title. It is a grabber that is hard for most people to pass without pausing to open the book to see if it is about protecting ducks in their natural habitat . . . *or what!* And once a prospective reader gets your creation in hand, hopefully he will know quickly that he can't live without it!

3. An Intriguing Beginning.

When do you write the beginning of a piece of exposition, a meditation?

Again, there is no hard and fast rule.

You may sit down and . . . immediately . . . the right "grabber" for your subject is there. It may come as you work with the material, so you form it from a mid-piece experience. Most of the time, it will probably be the *last* thing you write. Masters from Cicero to current word artists have found that, unless inspired earlier, it is best to write your manuscript and then study it for an answer to the question: "How can I interest my reader in this idea?"

THE MOST IMPORTANT WORDS you write in your entire manuscript will be the first few sentences. If you don't interest your reader in the beginning, as a published writer, he will thumb on to another article in the magazine or place your book back on the shelf. Even in writing for the people of your known world, this is important.

One of my friends made a copy of a letter my son had written. His first sentence was: "You told me it would be this way." In the next paragraphs, he structured a situation of life and, ultimately, brought it to the conclusion where her prophecy had come true. She was so delighted with the beginning that had held her in suspense through the letter, she wanted me to have a copy.

In all of your writing, work carefully on beginning. No matter how profound your thoughts, no matter how consistent your logic, no matter how beautiful your phrasing . . . a reader may never know . . . if you don't intrigue him IN THE BEGINNING.

Some devices you may consider are:

A. Puzzling Statement.

Charles Lamb opened a piece of writing with the cryptic remark: "I have no ears." Do you see how "catchy" that would be to a reader flipping through a magazine. You *have* to read at least the next sentence . . . and the next . . . and . . .

B. Startling statement.

"Baseball is a game that appeals to fools" is the beginning of an article that appeals to me because I agree with the premise; it appeals to my husband because he violently disagrees! Either reaction would cause us to want to read more.

C. Refer to History.

"During those dark nights of the Civil War, the nation's president prowled the White House corridors at night praying for guidance" begins a piece on prayer that I love. Interested in the events and personalities of the past, the writer "grabs" my interest by giving me a word picture of a historical event.

D. Quotation.

"Ask not what your country can do for you; ask what you can do for your country." Those who identify strongly with the philosophies of John Kennedy are immediately interested in a piece of writing that explores the familiar quote . . . whether favorably or unfavorably. The quote is a catcher.

E. Humor.

People love to laugh. If you can insert humor in your first sentences, your reader will probably be intrigued to read farther. This does not mean recapping a joke from the *Reader's Digest;* it has to be humor inherent within the piece itself. Study Erma Bombeck, Jean Kerr for this kind of attention-getter.

F. Illustration.

People are interested in people. When you begin your exposition, your meditation with a story, you are using a very strong interest-device indeed. My student who wrestled with contemporary problems perceived at The Helping Hand always began his work with real-life situations gleaned from the people in such a strategic locale for exposure to real-life drama.

G. Rhetorical Question.

One of the finest beginnings I have read is the first sentence of Bacon's essay "Of Truth." It is: "What is truth?" said jesting Pilate; and would not stay for an answer.

H. Personal Experience.

People are interested in *you!* When you can begin your writing with an experience out of your own life, you probably have your strongest tool. When forced to make a decision between a personal experience and a third-person illustration, it is a good rule to always choose the first even though the latter may be more dramatic. The first person is more intimate, more intriguing.

I. Top News Event.

Billy Graham is a master of this device in his public speaking. It works well in contemporary magazine writing, in current letter writing, but it is limited to that and, of course, newspapers. Because the top news event of today is totally forgotten tomorrow—certainly six months from now (which is the publication lapse of many magazines) . . . although it can be effective, use it with care. It "dates" your work and, therefore, limits your audience.

J. Unusual Structure.

"Dear Sir" . . . "Dear Diary" . . . Discussion with your cat . . . Letting a room in your house tell the story . . . and so on.

I structured my book *What I Will Tell My Children About God* on the device of exploring ideas with my children. So each chapter is "set up" as a dialogue with my sons.

Another book, *Portrait in a Nursery,* is set forth with the nursery itself as narrator. It details being an "extra" room to hold the ironing board and suitcases. Unimportant. Unloved. Drab. . . . And *then* things began to change: new paint, new curtains, new furniture. Why? Ultimately a new baby is brought in the room . . . and it understands its new importance: "I AM THE NURSERY!"

4. An Appropriate Structure.

For the body of your manuscript, you will want to choose the focal organizational format that will be most useful for your goal.

Some of these may be used as a single entity; other forms will be combined to produce your best communication. Listed below are some of the dominant patterns of expository expression available for your use.

A.   Personal Experience.

A person "thinking, evaluating, interpreting" a slice of life as he has lived it. An excellent example of this type of writing for you to study is the *Reader's Digest* "First Person" accounts. They range from epic proportions like "I Shot Down Yamamoto" to the unusual like "The Bear Who Came to Dinner" to the general "I Was Afraid to Have a Baby!" Combining narration, description, dialogue, and, perhaps, other forms, this is one of the most exciting structures of exposition-meditational sharing, but also one of the most demanding because it *is* a conglomerate of techniques rather than one central outline.

B.   Definition.

This is a structural format that is excellent for the exploration of abstract terms. When I taught Exposition, I had the class divide into small groups and share their manuscripts using this device. A boy had taken the topic of loneliness and given it his definition. This is an excerpt:

> Lonely is walking into a crowded classroom, squeezing in between gregarious people, and never being noticed. Lonely is carrying a tray into the chatter-clattering cafeteria, sitting at a table with laughing peers, and eating alone. Lonely is going to a basketball game, merging with the screaming mob, and never making a sound.

After the sharing group, I asked the students to write "reaction papers" to the one read. This is Margo's reaction to the above:

> I do not personally understand lonely. In fact, I never thought of the term until today. But as I listened to his voice and looked into his eyes, the poignancy of the definition of lonely attacked me. For the first time, I realized that it was a problem that the U.S.O. or the United Fund didn't take care of. Lonely was a problem in the world about ME. Maybe I'd better "sensitive up!"

Examples, cause and effect, and other format structures may augment the form of Definition. But, as indicated in this excerpt from the young man's paper, it can be solely the exploration of definition itself. And the effect of such structure may be seen in Margo's reaction.

Einstein used this form in an extended definition of religion in which he explored philosophically three types of religious feelings. Scientific definition may also be a format. Or the purely personal definition as given in the example of "lonely" . . . or in one I wrote on the definition of the "Cookie Jar" in my home . . . or the definition of the term "Let's Have a Coke!" when stated by my best friend. This is a strong form for many types of "thinking, interpreting, and evaluating life."

C. Protest.

This format uses the soundest form of logic of which you are capable. It simply is your statement of your views on something which, in your estimation, is deserving reform. It should contain fire, fervor, and hard-hitting reasoning. If you can make your readers react angrily, so much the better! You'll have readers, even if they read to disagree!

Strong catchy titles are especially useful with this format. "Keep Christmas Commercial!", "I Don't Believe God Heard Me Pray," "Down with Dogs!" are some of the titles I remember from "protest" writing. But remember that this is not solely argument which presents a case; this is exploration of an issue. There is a distinction between argumentation and "evaluating, interpreting life." . . . Keep that clear.

D. Description.

Although often used as a supporting device in another structural format, Description can stand as a form in its own right. Description, as such, is most useful in painting a word picture of something concrete, although its use is not restricted to what we can see and smell. We can describe abstract concepts and reactions to them. In its extreme forms, description is either objective or subjective . . . most of it will lie somewhere between the poles.

Here is an example of the form of Description.

There is stillness, a hush abroad as I touch the day at its beginning.
Neighbors' houses are silent; no cars pass at the end of the
lane. I hear the sound of a single bee among the marigolds,
and somewhere a cardinal sings.

A deep sense of oneness with nature and with all of living, a
quickening, widens horizons and lifts me to reach beyond
myself. . . . I will hear a kind of song within that sings for
hours or days and brings me secrets that do not fit into
words.

Jean Hersey
"Early Morning Magic"
Woman's Day

From this example, you can see that the first and most important job in any descriptive endeavor is the selection of details to
be included. The selection is made to form a single dominant impression so that the reader not only sees, hears, smells sensorially
the described experience, but also *feels* the abstract emotions.

A few well-chosen details are stronger than profusion. With
this format, economy of words is especially desirable. Rely heavily on nouns and verbs. Good description is a challenge to even
the most experienced writer. And one of the most enjoyable.

E. Comparison/Contrast.

From the beginning of our experience in life, we make comparisons and contrasts: my puppy is black but yours is white with
brown spots. But both are wiggly cuddly balls of puppy in stark
contrast to the superior sophistication of the gray tomcat who
lives down the street. This ability to observe similarities and
diversities forms a pattern of "interpreting life" that can be highly
successful. C. S. Lewis is a master of this structure. Study his
works.

When using this device, be careful to give your subjects similar
treatment. Points used for one should be used for the other and,
as a rule, in the same order. All points pertinent to comparison or
contrast should be explored in the same dimension.

Arrangement is decided by the purpose. If your purpose is

merely to point out likenesses or differences, your structure will be more balanced than if you are seeking to show superiority of one over another. This, of course, includes the technique of argument and, therefore, the manuscript may not be as equally balanced.

The structure may be used by portraying one view and then the other; after which your conclusion is made. A second use would be to present the comparing or contrasting views, point by point, followed with a joint summation.

Subjects I have seen strategically structured on this pattern include such things as: (a) religious college/secular college; (b) marriage alone/career alone; (c) marriage and career/marriage alone; (d) strengths given to children from father/from mother; (e) existentialism/Christianity, and so on.

F. *Advice.*

A person who "thinks, evaluates, and interprets life" often will have answers to the haunting "how to" questions that plague most people. I heard an untrue generalization on TV the other day, but it isn't as far wrong as it sounds. A book editor said: "You can publish anything if you put the words 'How To' in the title!"

People long to know *how to:* . . . make their home happy . . . keep their children's affection . . . control their emotions . . . acquire self-discipline . . . get along with in-laws . . . take care of houseplants . . . make candles . . . decorate cakes . . . install a stereo . . and on and on! I even have a book entitled *How to Marry a Minister!* I had been married to one for years before I bought the book . . and I have never read it . . . but it was such an intriguing title I couldn't leave the bookstore without it!

Included in this pattern of exposition will probably be arguments, illustrations, and some rules of "do's and don'ts." Although a conglomerate of technique, it is a form that has a high value in sharing with your family, your friends, or other readers who seek wisdom you have gained. It is a polished statement of your position and demands much self-knowledge. It is useful for writer *and* reader.

G. *Classification.*

Writers are usually "born classifiers." We face a world of so much detail and activity that, to cope, our brain naturally begins to sift through, divide, classify, and examine in orderly fashion. Charles Colson, a trained attorney, said that when he first encountered Christianity, he tried to classify his thoughts in two categories: Pro and Con. Thus, in a logical, forward moving manner, he could set down, according to thesis, the myriad of thoughts and arguments that came to his mind.

One of the best discussions of the Vietnam war I have read used this structure. The author used the orderly basis of classifying the categories of problems: economic, political, military, et cetera. Thus he handled a complex topic . . . in which many authors get bogged in the quicksand of too many considerations . . . with clarity, lucidity, and a forward march to his final point. He could do so because of the organization of classification.

H. *Life Vignette.*

This structure is usually succinct yet graceful; subtle yet with the point crystal clear; tender without being sentimental. It is a person "thinking, evaluating, interpreting life" in a way that strikes a responsive chord in the heart of the reader. This is the kind of exposition, meditation, that is carried in purses, wallets, and posted on bulletin boards.

Marjorie Holmes wrote a delightful piece on the familiar shout, "Mother, I'm Home!" She traced it through life from kindergarten into her children's marriages:

> They grow up so fast they go away one by one. After a while, only on visits does that glad cry come. . . . Home is somewhere else. A different job, a different life, a different love to follow yours, a different person to greet them when they return . . . and that once-familiar cry has taken on a new significance. . . . You don't have to worry. They have reached their destination. Each one is safely in. In a new and much more wonderful way, each voice is assuring you: "I'm home, Mother, I'm home!"

Probably my most published piece of writing is a letter I wrote to my parents the night before my wedding. It is a specifically detailed portrait of the gifts they had given to me. People have shown me clippings of it in many states. One of my friends found a copy of it in a scrapbook of her mother's in England. My brother found it reprinted in an Italian magazine he bought at an airport in Rome.

The Life Vignette is one of the most treasured formats of writing exposition, meditations. The major caution is to avoid sentimentality. Stay close to the vivid, the real, the honest.

I. Narration.

Narration is the factual or fictional report of a sequence of events. It may include description, dialogue, and other technical tools. It may stand alone.

In "thinking, evaluating, and interpreting life," often objective narrative reporting is strongest when used alone. The reporting of the sequence of events of the evacuation from Vietnam, after the U.S. withdrawal, was done concisely, objectively, and effectively by one of my students who had worked in one of the camps to which refugees came.

There are problems in pure narration. Some of these are: Selection of details . . . time order . . . transitions . . . point of view . . . and dialogue. All of these must be used economically and with a constant focus on the *point* of narration which is communicating ideas.

J. Inspiration.

Although not a technical pattern, the writer specifically concerned with the triplet of writing for self, for God, for others will want to explore this specific. It is a conglomerate of personal experience, advice, description, narration, or definition as a rule. But it is a *type* of "thinking, evaluating, interpreting life" that beams on a single theme. Symbolism may be used as in John Kord Lagemann's "Bring It to the Rainbow" where he talked about "the glow that crowns an all-out effort to do any kind of job." Epigrams may be used as my mother's oft-repeated statement in a piece I wrote: "Use your misfortunes as stepping stones to happy things."

Whatever devices or combination of devices used, the writer is perusing life in a way that is inspiring to the highest in both himself and in those who read.

K. *Analogy*.

Although a type of comparison, analogy deserves special consideration because it performs a special service. In the structure of analogy, the writer may present something abstract or difficult to comprehend by showing its likeness to something concrete or easy to understand. This is an unusually efficient means of giving meaning to hard-to-grasp ideas.

There is a warning that should go to the beginning writer of analogy: Don't ever use the pattern in logical argument. It should never be offered as proof. Analogy has its principal function in its ability to *explain*.

An example of this structure of meditation is one where the writer is attempting to cope with the "Why?" of the death of a small child in an automobile accident. He shows the likeness of the situation to the time when an earthquake is forming in the bowels of the earth which will ultimately bring death and destruction. But the God Who deliberately limited His power to allow us to live in a world of natural law does nothing to squelch the embryonic earthquake. It happens as natural disaster. The author, then, makes his point that, given a mechanized society, the God Who deliberately limits His power to allow mankind free choice should do nothing to stop the automobile accident that took the life of the small child.

L. *Character Sketch*.

One of the most exciting forms is the character sketch. This enables a person "thinking, evaluating, interpreting life" to make his point as it is actually lived. I have often maintained that I cannot understand many theological points of doctrine through verbiage. But if you will let me see it lived in human existence, I begin to comprehend.

The thing to remember in the "Character Sketch" is total honesty so that the character you describe is whole . . . complete with warts and weaknesses. The "flat" characters described simply to make one point lack credibility and if your goal is serious, you will fail. "Flat" characters are used for humor . . . and we love the exaggerated point the author is trying to make. . . . But if you are doing a true character sketch, strive to make your character well-rounded so that we see humanity as it is.

The *Reader's Digest* "My Most Unforgettable Character" section will offer many examples of this art at its best. William Allen White's tribute to his daughter, Mary, is a classic you may want to study.

This form you will want to use prolifically in your personal life: birthday, anniversaries, retirements, tributes, et cetera.

M. Process Analysis.

This pattern sets forth the chronology of achieving a certain goal. A form of narration, it is specifically an entity because it deals with *process*. Narration is concerned with a story—a general concept; meditation, by process analysis, is concerned with the *steps* involved—the specifics.

One of the best pieces using this pattern I have read was one done for a class assignment by a young man who explained his selection of a college. Step by step, he went through the process of exploring the various possibilities, his reasoning in regard to the merits and deficiencies of each, and his ultimate resolution.

He could have told it as a story (using narration) he could have defined "college" in terms of his personal desires; he could have classified the types of college available; he could have compared and contrasted colleges; he could have described colleges . . . but for his goal of leading people to share in his reasoning through the *process* of college-selection, he chose process analysis. It was his strongest tool.

N. Example.

The device of exposition, meditation, by example serves four major purposes: (a) amplifying a statement which might otherwise have been unimpressively brief; (b) proving an original statement; (c) a means of lending interest to a generalized statement; (d) a means of conveying more specific knowledge.

This is the general category of which the Character Sketch is a segment. My statement that I can best understand theology when I can see it *lived* is true in more facets of experience that one person's life. John Stuart Mill, in striving to prove the fallacy of a cliché, used multiple examples of history to prove his point.

But, indeed the dictum that truth always triumphs over persecution, is one of those pleasant falsehoods which men repeat after one another till they pass into commonplaces, but which all experience refutes. History teems with instances of truth put down by persecution. If not suppressed forever, it may be thrown back for centuries. To speak only of religious opinions: the Reformation broke out at least twenty times before Luther, and was put down. Arnold of Bresica was put down. Fra Dolcino was put down. Savonarola was put down. The Albigeois were put down. The Vaudois were put down. The Lollards were put down. The Hussites were put down. . . . Persecution has always succeeded save where the heretics were too strong a party to be effectually persecuted.

The organization of the pattern of example usually moves from the general to the particular (as in Mill's pieces) or the reverse: from the particular to the general (draw word pictures of the specific from which a general conclusion is drawn). Since the purpose of this device is to support, to reinforce, and to clarify, examples should lead either *from* or *to* the topic sentences of paragraphs.

Basically, all of Jesus's parables may be said to be exposition by example. When, in my life, I have *had* to know what God is like, how comforting to leave theology and go to the specific example of the loving Father welcoming his prodigal son . . . and know that Jesus said: "God is *like that!*" Example is a powerful tool for clarifying and explaining.

Most of us can understand theology or philosophy when we can see it *lived!*

O.   Induction/Deduction.

Usually these forms are used in argument, so it may be surprising to think of them as forming an effective pattern for "interpreting life." But it is useful here.

Induction or deduction may be developed simply as explanation of the author's "thoughts, interpretations, and/or evaluations" . . . without the effort (made in argumentation) to prove this the *only* way to think, interpret, or evaluate!

Induction can be defined as the reasoning *from* particular facts of individual cases to a general conclusion. In a simplified form, it can be likened to a lawyer presenting all the specifics of his evidence against an accused person . . . and then he asks the jury to make the "inductive leap" to the generalization that the accused did commit the crime. The generalization has its basis in the specifics.

Deduction, on the other hand, is the reasoning from the general *to* the specific . . . or from a premise *to* a logical conclusion. Deduction may be outlined thus:

> *Major Premise* (General conclusion): Attendance in a graduate seminar is the only requirement for an "A."
> *Minor Premise* (The specific that fits into the generalization): I have attended every session of the graduate seminar.
> *Conclusion:* I will make an "A" in the seminar.

Both induction and deduction are highly logical processes, and any element of weakness in reasoning can totally undermine a meditation or exposition dependent upon the reasoning process. Be very careful, when using this device, that you do not use flimsy evidence (subjective opinion, gossip, or analogy, none of which can hold up a generalization; instead use verified facts and authoritative opinion) and that you do not use too little evidence for your audience. Although, with a small amount of evidence, you might obtain my understanding of your belief that there *is* a God . . . you would have to marshall a great deal more power to gain that comprehension from an avowed agnostic.

It is best, when using this pattern, to always assume a skeptical audience. A believer in the Report of the Warren Commission, it takes hard evidence for a writer to even gain my attention . . . much less my acceptance . . . of the position that it is not accurate. Always take the stance that your reading audience will want to know the logical basis for all generalizations and conclusions.

P. Cause and Effect.

This is the form which seeks to present your conclusions of "thought, interpretation, and evaluation" in an answer to the "why" of things. To fully explain the causes of teenage runaways in our nation demands the writer seek not only immediate causes (the ones first confronted) but also ultimate causes (the fundamental underlying reasons which explain the obvious ones).

There is an important need for this kind of writing. How else can root problems be grappled with? The immediate cause of a teen-age runaway in my neighborhood may be a premarital pregnancy, but the runaway itself may be attributed to the unfriendly rela-tionships within her home, which may be traced even further backward to the family's break with the church. David Wilkerson has produced some excellent writing on this topic, where he explicates his belief that home problems compose the root prob-lems of the nation's current teen dilemmas.

Some confusions many writers have with this type of exposi-tion, meditation, are: (a) assuming a cause/effect relationship that is not valid (example: a student failed my course in college and told his parents it was because he did not turn in the term paper); (b) not considering all possibly relevant factors before attributing causes (when the parents called me, I told them that the term-paper grade was one of twenty grades in my book, all of which were zero because *nothing* had been turned in!); (c) not supporting the analysis by more than mere assertions; (always *offer evidence!*); (d) not being honest and objective. Old preju-dices or acceptance of clichés will destroy this type of analysis for any thinking reader.

Although this can be used very formally in logical writing, it is also a pattern that can be used informally and personally. I think you'll enjoy the following example of the latter use of Cause/ Effect written by Jill Hurley.

It is a cool October night in the year 1946. Mother begins to feel pains, and wonders if it is indigestion. At 10:30 o'clock a child is born. In the beginning God created; in the now God creates. I BELIEVE.
Five years old and I hear the church bell ringing, calling us to Sunday school. We sing "Climb, climb up sunshine moun-tain." We fold our hands and bow our heads in prayer, then listen as the teacher reads us stories of Noah and Abraham and Moses. I BELIEVE.
A second grader now and our little family packs up and moves to the West Coast for a year. Homesick for Ohio. One bright morning I go to the door. "Mom, Dad—Aunt Mary's here!" I BELIEVE.

Someone is reading the "Lost and Found" column of our evening newspaper. Next day a little yellow kitten is brought to school and I run joyfully all the way home. "Mom, Mom, someone has found Buttercup! Take good care of him—I'm going back to school." I BELIEVE.

It is Palm Sunday, and I am twelve years old. The service comes to a close and the invitation hymn is played. I walk forward to the front of the church with joy in my heart and tears in my eyes. The Heavenly Father adopts me into His family and calls me "daughter." I hear the minister ask, "Do you believe—?" I BELIEVE. . . .

Twelfth grade, and I am a "mighty senior." Our gym class is quieted while an announcement is made: "President Kennedy has been assassinated." No, please, no! Our country is thrown into shock by something that is supposed to happen only in history books. Lyndon Johnson appears before his countrymen saying, "With God's help . . ." I BELIEVE. . . .

It is July 20, 1969. Neil Armstrong has just set foot on the moon—and we are able to watch him do it. The astronauts return safely home. God is! I BELIEVE.

It is Sunday, and we are at worhsip. We partake of holy communion. We remember the greatest moment in the history of mankind, when the Son of the living God was crucified, nailed to a cross. But now—He lives! I BELIEVE!

5. Effective Anecdotes.

An anecdote may be defined as "usually short narrative of an interesting, amusing, or curious incident, often biographical and generally characterized by human interest." Writer Harry Edward Neal said that an anecdote is "a brief story involving people in action."

An anecdote fulfills my most frequently written admonition on beginning writers' papers: SHOW ME! DON'T TELL ME! The *Reader's Digest*—with its art-of-living articles and its features of short anecdotes taken from the real-life arena—is an excellent source. Establish a file of subject-marked anecdotes (a separate

shoe box) and you will always have these enriching additions to
your writing at your fingertips.

The use of quotes will also be an asset. They validate your arguments; they add charm and substance; they frequently will succinctly capsulize your entire piece.

Quotes may be found in books, newspapers, personal interviews, tapes, records, and, most easily, in some of the most pithy
reference books. Every writer should have a complete Shakespeare, Emerson's essays, Lord Chesterfield's *Letters to His Son,*
copies of Ruskin, C. S. Lewis, and other favorite philosophers,
plus as many books of quotations as possible. Bartlett's is the best
known, but there are countless others . . . many in paperback.
The Bible, of course, is frequently your best source . . . both ar-
tistically and authoritatively.

6. A Forceful Conclusion.

There is no magic formula for the forceful conclusion . . . just
as there is none for a dynamic beginning. You have to study your
manuscript, your ideas, and work until you can find a conclusion
that fully satisfies. That is vague . . . but probably the best that
can be done . . . the beginning must intrigue; the conclusion
must satisfy.

One way to learn the art of conclusion-writing is to study good
pieces of exposition, meditations, in magazines. Study their structure, their building, their rounding off. Compare these with newspaper conclusions. Got the difference? It's easy to spot. Newspaper articles don't have conclusions. They end. But . . . a good
piece of writing creatively always concludes with a solid bang! An
oomph! That is one of the important differences in journalism
and creation.

The goal of journalism is to report facts with the most interesting first. When that reportage is completed, the goal is achieved.
Period.

The goal of writing effectively is to create an entity: a viable
"something" that has a beginning, builds in force to a climax, and
concludes in a way that is aesthetically pleasing. Then, there is
wholeness . . . unity . . . in the creation. The *art* has arrived.

As with the beginning of your meditation, I can offer a list of tools that are helpful in making forceful conclusions. These, plus others you may add through the years, will help you "satisfy" your reader in all your written sharing.

Some devices are:

A. The Summarizing Quote.

A beautiful character sketch of Oscar Hammerstein concluded with this summarizing quote from the man himself:

> "I know the world is filled with trouble and many injustices," he once said, "but reality is as beautiful as it is ugly. I think it is just as important to sing about beautiful mornings as it is to talk about slums. I just couldn't write anything without hope in it!"

B. The Quote and Booster.

This is a conclusion where you find a quote that almost does it . . . but not quite! . . . so you add a few words of your own to add the oomph! One I like is a piece of writing on the rewards of jogging, which pulls one out of the mechanical haze into which industrialization can throw us. Here is the conclusion:

> Victor Hugo said: "To reform a man, you must begin with his grandmother!" Well, grandchildren, you've just been saved from robot-ville! The reformation in your genes has already begun!

C. The Anecdotal Ending.

An example of this device in use is in an essay I wrote entitled "Cushioned by Gratitude" where I discussed the life truth that many of our problems come because of false expectations, unreasonable demands, a refusal to face *what is* with faith. In its conclusion, I drew a word picture of my active mother who was stricken in her late life with Parkinson's Disease. She, ultimately, had to enter a nursing home, was submitted to a wheelchair, faced total blindness. In the face of such adversity, she remained radiant, loving, lovable.

I concluded the article with this anecdote.

> "One of the last times I talked to Mother, I asked how she managed to be so triumphant and joyful in the midst of a problem-littered life. She did not hesitate for an answer."

"Oh, honey, I had passed my allotted three-score years and ten before I came here [to the nursing home]. These are bonus years —bonus years with my husband, with my children. Because of that, they are *good* years."

"But you are bound to have periods of unhappiness at the loss of your home, your sight, your health—"

She nodded.

"Yes, there are pangs of unhappiness, but they are always *cushioned by gratitude:* gratitude for a husband whose love never fails; gratitude for God, who has walked through all of life's changing seasons with me and who grows dearer each day! Even under less-than-ideal conditions I find life to be very *good* when cushioned by gratitude!"

D.   The Split-anecdotal Ending.

This is one of the most effective devices available, but difficult to come by. Only rarely will you find an anecdote that will allow you to create full circle. An example of this power in action is from this exposition on "Divorce" given by Jack Rogers:

[Rogers' introduction] It was the morning of December twenty-fourth. The day before Christmas. Outside the courthouse the lawn was hidden by a thick coverlet of snow. The branches of the trees were heavy and white. Somewhere down the hall from the courtroom where I was sitting, a radio was sending forth the voices of singers, telling of a "Silent Night, Holy Night," reminding us that this evening we would commemorate the birth of Christ, who taught us of peace on earth, and good will toward men.

It would be a family night. Parents and children would gather in spacious living rooms and cozy parlors, drawn closer together by the warmth of the Holy Season: singing hymns, giving gifts, and rejoicing in the Saviour's birth.

But now it was morning. I was sitting on a hard, straight-backed chair, and there were five other people in the big, bare room. The woman who was sitting near the center of the room was wearing a Christmassy red dress, but it was completely incongruous with the drab atmosphere of the court. The judge listened quietly as the woman told of her nervousness and loss of weight. In a few moments, the plaintiff's sister followed her to the stand and answered a few simple questions. The lawyer then dropped his papers into his briefcase and walked across the courtroom and into the hall. The two women followed, the woman in the red dress dabbing at her eyes with a much-wrinkled handkerchief she held clutched in her hand.

There was no sound but the voices of the carolers as they finished the last verse of "Silent Night." And there was no movement except that of the judge's hand as he signed the decree.

What had happened? Nothing very unusual. A woman had received a divorce. A family had been separated. It happens very day. Even the day before Christmas, that special day when a family wishes to be together. . . .

[Rogers' conclusion] I didn't personally know the woman in the Christmassy dress who sat across the courtroom from me on December twenty-fourth last year. But I can well imagine how she and the defendant, her husband, must have looked in a far different setting. In a small chapel, fresh with the fragrance of flowers just cut, the rustle of new satin and lace, and two people's faces flushed with happiness, as they repeat after the minister the familiar lines . . . "for better, for worse, for richer, for poorer, in sickness, in health, till death do us part."

We must think and pray before those vows are taken. If we realize our obligations to ourselves and to society; if we are forewarned of the dangers of carelessness; if we know what marriage really means; then . . . "what God hath joined together," no man will put asunder.

Not today, nor tomorrow, nor the day before Christmas.

> From "The Day Before Christmas"
> in Charles J. Steward and H. Bruce
> Kendall *On Speeches and Speakers,*
> Holt, Rinehart and Winston, 1968.

E.   The Piece of Poetry.

For that added "oomph" that summarizes in already well-stated words, sometimes poetry will be the best form. On a meditation calling for deeper human understanding, I concluded with a bit of poetry I had heard my mother quote through my life:

If I could only see the road you came
The jagged rocks and crooked way . . .
I would more kindly think of your mis-step
And only praise!
If I could know the heartache you have felt
The longings for the things that never came . . .
I would more kindly judge your erring then
Nor even blame!

F.   The Echo Ending.

This effective tool is used when you select a key word or phrase that is used throughout your manuscript and, ultimately, weave it into the final sentence. For example, in my book, *No Matter the Weather,* I concluded each chapter with the phrase: "No Matter the Weather." . . . It emphasized the whole point I was trying to make of God's Presence with His child in *All* seasons . . . and the last words written was that overarching refrain or phrase.

G.   Final Statement by the Author.

This can be structured logically, formally, emotionally, informally . . . whatever is the most satisfying "rounding out" of your exposition.

For example, in my book, *Even When I Cry,* the final paragraph consists of a succinct summation of what I believe is God's Truth. I wrote: "Through His Word He tells us, 'I know you—as you are! I know the reason behind each failure and each success of your life. I know the consequences of each of those events. You do not have to explain yourself to Me. I already know all about you. I know all that is good. I know all that is bad. I am by your side when you laugh with joy and hold life closely to your heart. I am with you when you suffer heartbreak. I stand, with loving arms outstretched to welcome you into my love, EVEN WHEN YOU CRY.' "

Study the conclusions of meditations that satisfy you best. Analyze their structure, their source of content, their technique. Internalize what "rounds off" a piece of writing . . . then trust yourself.

18

THE WRITING OF POETRY

Stephen Spender wrote: "I dread writing poetry . . . a poem is a terrible journey . . . the writing of a poem brings one face to face with one's own personality with all its familiar and clumsy limitations. In every other phase of existence, one can exercise the orthodoxy of a conventional routine. . . . In poetry, one is wrestling with a god."

Emily Dickinson wrote:

> To hear an oriole sing
> May be a common thing,
> Or only a divine.
>
> The fashion of the ear
> Attireth that it hear
> In dun or fair.
>
> It is not of the bird
> Who sings the same, unheard,
> As unto crowd.
>
> So whether it be rune,
> Or whether it be none,
> Is of within;
>
> The "tune is in the tree,"
> The skeptic showeth me;
> "No, sir! In thee!"

I found this entry in my Journal in a self-discussion of poetry:
"If you tell me the way you see it rather than the way it is, then
this helps me to more fully discover the way I see it. . . . If I tell
you the way I see it (knowing that may be far from the way it is),
at least my thoughts help to stimulate you to more fully discover
the way *you* see it . . . so in our mutual pursuit of writing, we
discover the answers to

I

Why?

You.

Who?

And, in the discovery, explode with the joyous fact:

We.

"Whee!"

Elizabeth Drew wrote that "the poet is neither an intellectual
nor an emotional being alone; he feels his thoughts and thinks his
sensations." And as such a being, I would define poetry as the
personal

singing
sighing
hoping
hating
faithful
fearful beat of one person's unique experience.

Wordsworth phrased it much more definitively in the Preface
to his second edition of *Lyrical Ballads*. He wrote:

"What is a Poet? To whom does he address himself? And
what language is to be expected from him? He is a man
speaking to men;

(Do you feel an urgency to articulate your thoughts to others? Do
you feel you have something to *say?* If so, you're a poet!)

"a man, it is true, endowed with more lively sensitivity,

(Are you, by nature, more sensitive than the average person around you?)

"more enthusiasm,

(Do you have higher highs . . . lower lows? An artist once made the simile that a creative person is as different in spirit from the average man as a race horse is to the plow horse.)

"and tenderness,

(Does your heart flood with love of life, beauty, people . . . ?)

"and a more comprehensive soul

(Is there a constant intensity to understand spiritual laws and realities . . . an unrelenting thirst for truth?)

"than are supposed to be common among mankind; a man pleased with his own passions and volition, and who rejoices more than other men in the spirit of life that is in him;

(Do you enjoy being alone? Do you enjoy long periods of solitary contemplative thought within yourself?)

"delighting to contemplate similar volitions and passions as manifested in the goings-on of the Universe, and habitually impelled to create them where he does not find them.

(Are you insatiably curious about how the world fits together in the God/man relationship, the man/man relationship?)

"To these qualities he has added a disposition to be affected more than other men by absent things as if they were present;

(Can you be deeply affected by thoughts, ideas, philosophies, stories, imaginations, theologies set forth in books or letters without a tangible relationship?)

"and an ability of conjuring up in himself passions and from practice, he has acquired a greater readiness and power in expressing what he thinks and feels, and especially those thoughts and feelings which, by his own choice or from the structure of his own mind, arise in him without immediate external excitement."

In the same volume, Wordsworth wrote of poetry:

"Poetry is the spontaneous overflow of powerful feelings;

(Although I had taken numerous courses in the techniques of writing poetry, it had never been a form I chose for my own use until Bill's critical illness in 1969. In that hospital room, when every corpuscle of my being was focused on his efforts to take the next breath, I found that I had to express myself . . . but my emotions were so powerful they could not be put into prose. Somehow only the compression of poetry could house my thoughts. They were too strongly focused for the wide lens of any structure other than poetry.)

"it takes its origin from emotion collected in tranquility: the emotion is contemplated till, by a species of reactions, the tranquility gradually disappears, and an emotion, kindred to that which was before the subject of contemplation, is gradually produced, and does itself actually exist in the mind."

At 4:30 P.M., May 25, 1973, my father died.
At 4:30 P.M., June 25, 1973, I wrote this poem whose origin was "from emotion collected in tranquility."

Daddy, once you said that if God willed you might,
As did Methuselah, live longer than nine hundred years;
I smiled wistfully at the thought.
Stay long upon this earth, Daddy.
Leave only when you must . . . not for your, but for our, sake.

Daddy, one month ago this hour you went away.
I was not there, but the nurse told me
How friends stood round your bed and
The doctor said you were a beautiful man.
When I dashed in a few hours later,
Somehow his recognition of your beauty
Made me more able to endure
Your inevitable leaving.

Daddy, I picked your casket with care:
a beautiful grey with blue velvet lining.
I selected your new suit: the one I bought you
For your ninetieth birthday. I realized it would
Be my last gift.

I was working on the structure of the service
When they told me I could see you.
I walked to the room, very serious.
The suit was lovely with the blue shirt,
The wide navy tie.
Your hands were resting quiet, familiar.
I touched them,
    Remembering how they had rumpled my hair;
    Decorated my Christmas trees;
    Painted my doll bed;
    Buried my cats;
    Fixed my bicycle flats;
    Rocked my babies; rumpled their hair;
    Fixed their bicycle flats.
I looked at your face
And found not you,
But your shell,
And I let you go
For the first time.
Flowers and relations kept coming:
Chrysanthemums and carnations and arranged red roses,
My tall, sober-faced brothers; my tearful sisters;
Alien, never-seen cousins and nephews, children become adults,
Placed helter-skelter about the rooms,
Settling themselves here and there,
Pulling from purses and wallets
Photographs implicating you
With their lives.

Daddy, it was a celebration and everyone laughed
And kept watching to see if I stayed strong
Which would make them so.
Food was brought in abundance:

A roasted beef was sliced; a carrot cake; custard pies.
Joe told how you taught him to milk a cow;
We went into gales of laughter
When he told about Lyman running over him with the car
When he walked with you and the cow;
I found a scrapbook in which Mother had penned
Numerous chapters of the Bible Joe had memorized
And I challenged him to quote them now;
He amazed us by doing so;
Then he challenged me to sing
The Sixty-Six Books of the Bible and I did.
He joined in half-way and we finished,
Breathless and laughing.

Outside the sun was shining.

And someone was sitting in your chair
At the table's head.

More people came.
The rooms bulged with stories of things you had said;
Sermons you had preached; times you had laughed.
A detached part of me listened to it all and thought:
Were I to write a paper on this rhetoric,
The predominant theme would be easy to find:
The strength of the man; his goodness.
The doctor had said: "Beautiful."
Perhaps that was the best word.

Daddy, flowers were everywhere.

I sat with the family looking at the blue-velvet lined coffin
In which your body lay. I could see your bald head
And my body
Wheezed
With the pain of separation.
The minister said he discovered, in forty-eight years of
    friendship,
That your chief characteristics
Were strength and wisdom.

I looked at him gratefully.

He knew you well.

Strength and wisdom, he said.
"Goodness" was engraved on your tombstone.
The doctor had called you "Beautiful."
Perhaps the words all fit.
We knew the man.
Daddy, your friends walked by your coffin slowly.
They didn't want to let you go.
Your children waited until the last.
We all knew there was a reservoir of
Strength and goodness
Wisdom and beauty
Leaving our lives
Incomplete.

I was the last.
I waited until everyone else had gone.
Summoning more strength than ever before in my life,
I stood and walked to the front where your body lay.
I touched your hands.
"I love you, Daddy," I whispered.
"I love you."
I looked at your face, trying to indelibly
Impress its features forever on my mind.
"Thank you, Daddy," I said finally. "Thank you for everything."
And, for the last time,
I let you go.

In the family room, I walked to a window where I could
Stand apart. Joe came and took me in his arms. We cried
Together. We had loved you special.
And you knew.

The cars were driving down the driveway.
I was in the second one, recollecting other days,
When we broke speed limits to make trains and buses;
The blue police car with the red flashing on its roof

Was guiding us to where your shell would rest.
We drove slowly and I pondered how many times in my life
I had ridden that road with you. You usually recounted
Stories of your boyhood at Center Grove, tales of the farm,
Beginnings of your ministry. And we laughed at your
Wry way of story-telling.
Now we were making the trip with you
For the last time.

Today, you have been gone one month.
I held your Bible and read some of the marked phrases
That had mattered in your life . . .
And I wondered if you'd really gone from our world . . .

Then, looking up, I saw the picture of your three tall sons;
I saw a picture of my children; I looked long at a picture
Of you with a little girl on your knee;
I used to be
That little girl . . .
And suddenly I felt the essence of YOURSELF
In all of us.

So I whisper once again: "Thank you, Daddy.
"Thank you for being strong and wise . . . good and
beautiful . . .
All in one person. At one time.
Thank you for striving to make your children, your grandchildren
Strong and wise . . . good and beautiful . . .
And when you felt satisfied,
Thank you for the way you chose to go.
"I love you, Daddy. I'll try to make you proud."

Wordsworth said: "Poetry is the spontaneous overflow of powerful feeling: it takes its origin from emotion collected in tranquility." He also said it was written by a person who, "from practice,
has acquired a greater readiness and power in expressing what he
thinks and feels."

I think I not only saw that concept of "emotion collected in
tranquility" most clearly when I wrote this poem a month removed from the time, but I also understood Wordsworth's de-

scription of the poet and his worth to others . . . more clearly.
For I sent a copy of the poem immediately to my brother who is
now a retired colonel from the United States Army. Having
served in combat in World War II, Korea, and two hitches in Vietnam, it is difficult for him to express his emotions. When he received my poem, he called immediately and said: "Thank you for
the release. That is what I *felt,* but I couldn't find the words to
say it!"

And I realized, as never before, the value of poets. They can
articulate compressed powerful emotion that brings release to the
persons who have not the power of words at their own command.

Have you recognized yourself in the description of a poet?
Have you felt the urge to write the "stuff of poetry" which can be
such a release valve for those who are not "word people?"

Good!

Now comes the hard work.

Sassoon, the great poet, said: "A man may be a born poet, but
he has to make himself an artist as well. He must master the instrument."

Note that last sentence.

Poetry means that you must *master* all the ways of "putting
words togther effectively" that have been discussed: rules,
figures of speech, sound effects, basic principles. And, in addition,
you must learn the techniques of the poetic form.

You may need to get a book that deals only with poetry for
you to understand the uses of metrics and forms. Succinctly, I
will set down the fundamentals here.

Basic definitions are:

METER: rhythm in verse; measured, patterned arrangement of
   syllables, primarily according to stress and length.
FOOT: a group of syllables serving as a unit of meter in verse;
   especially, such a unit having a specified placement of the
   stressed / sound in combination with one or two unstressed
   sounds.[11]
There may be as many as nine feet in the meter of a line.
METRICAL FEET are labeled:

IAMB (Adjective: IAMBIC): first syllable unstressed ˘
second stressed ´ .

EXAMPLES: Ăr ránge . . . Sŭr páss . . . tŏ níght

TROCHEE (Adjective: TROCHAIC): first syllable
stressed ´ second unstressed ˘ .

EXAMPLES: Thír tў . . . Éas tĕr . . . Gláth lў

ANAPEST (Adjective: ANAPESTIC): first two syllables
unstressed ˘ ; third stressed ´ .

EXAMPLES: Sŭ pĕr séde . . . Ĭn tĕr rúpt . . .
Căr ŏ líne

DACTYL (Adjective: DACTYLIC): first syllable
stressed ´ ; second and third unstressed ˘ .

EXAMPLES: Rég ŭ lăr . . . Mí nĭ mĭze . . .
Háp pĭ lў

There are exceptional metrical feet which can be used for effect. Beginning poets need to learn the discipline of working within the regular feet unless there is a special effect they are striving to achieve. If you want to be an artist of words, said Sassoon, you must *master the instrument*.

Some exceptional feet are:

AMPHIBRACH: Unstressed syllable first ˘ ; stressed
syllable second ´ ; Unstressed syllable third ˘ .

AMPHIMACER: Stressed syllable first ´ ; unstressed
syllable second ˘ ; stressed syllable third ´ .

TRUNCATION: Unstressed syllable deleted from the
first iamb in an iambic line - / .

CATALEXIS: The last unstressed syllable is dropped

from the last trochee in a trochaic line - / .

SPONDEE: Two stressed syllables // .

PYRHHUS: Two unstressed syllables ᴗᴗ.

CAESURA: Pauses determined by the sense and grammar

of the line // .

In addition to the names of metrical feet . . . and the rhythm
. . . you should know the names for poetic lines. These are given
according to the number of feet within a specific line.

Names for Lines

MONOMETER: One foot in a line. A foot is marked __/

DIMETER: Two feet in a line. Marked __/ /

TRIMETER: Three feet in a line. Marked __/ / /

TETRAMETER: Four feet in a line. Marked __/ / / /

PENTAMETER: Five feet in a line. Marked __/ / / / /

HEXAMETER: Six feet in a line. Marked __/ / / / / /

HEPTAMETER: Seven feet in a line. Marked __/ / / / / / /

OCTOMETER: Eight feet in a line. Marked __/ / / / / / / /

NONAMETER: Nine feet in a line. Marked __/ / / / / / / / /

One other important word for you to have in your vocabulary
is SCANSION: The marking of feet in a line of poetry.

An example of Scansion would be:

With rav/ ished ears/	Iambic Dimeter line
The mon /arch hears,/	Iambic Dimeter line
As sumes/ the god,/	Iambic Dimeter line
Af fects/ to nod,/	Iambic Dimeter line
And seems/ to shake/ the spheres. /	Iambic Trimeter line

If you need a fuller discussion of meter, you will find it in any book on poetry in your library. For the major fundamentals of rhyme, refer back to the chapter on sound effects.

Some other terms and definitions are the MAJOR VERSE FORMS.

COUPLET: Two lines linked by rhyme.

Each end rhyme in a poem is marked with a letter of the alphabet.

EXAMPLE: With ravished ears   a
            The monarch hears   a
            Assumes the god,   b
            Affects to nod,   b
            And seems to shake the spheres.   c
            In the couplet, the
                rhyme is marked   a
                                         a in the first couplet;
                                         b
                                         b in the second couplet,
                                              et cetera

TERCET: Three lines bound by rhyme.

Normally, the tercet
        is marked: a
                            a
                            a for the first
                                tercet;   b
                                             b
                                             b in the second ter-
                                                  cet, et cetera

A variation of rhyming words in the tercet is called the TERZA RIMA which is a three-line stanza whose rhyme endings are   aba
            bcb
            cdc, et cetera

QUATRAIN: a four-line stanza which may have any rhyme scheme. The most common use of the Quatrain is the BAL-

LAD STANZA whose rhyme scheme is abcb. The most common example:

Roses are red	a
Violets are blue	b
Sugar is sweet	c
And so are you	b

QUINTET: A five-line stanza of a variety of rhyme schemes.

SESTET: a six-line stanza of a variety of rhyme schemes.

SEPTET: a seven-line stanza of a variety of rhyme schemes, the most common of which is RIME ROYAL whose rhyme scheme is ababbcc.

OCTAVE: an eight-line stanza of a variety of rhyme schemes.

SPENSERIAN STANZA: nine-line stanza, the first eight Iambic Pentameter; the ninth Iambic Hexameter rhyming ababbcbcc.

An example of rhyme-scheme markings can be seen in this Spenserian stanza taken from Edmund Spenser's *The Faerie Queene:*

Like as / a ship, / that through /   5 feet

the o / cean wyde /   a Iambic Pentameter lines

Directs / her course / unto / one

'cer / taine cost, /   b

Is met / of ma / ny a coun / ter

winde / and tyde, /   Third foot: anapest

                                             a

With which / her wing / ed

speed / is let / and crost, /

And she / her selfe / in   **b**

storme / surges tost; /   Last foot: amphimacer

Yet mak / ing ma / ny a borde, /

and ma / ny a bay, /   Third; last: anapest

                          c

Still win / neth way, / nor

hath / her com / pass lost: /   **b**

Right so / it fares / with me /

in this / long way, /   **c**

Whose course / is of / ten

stayd, / yet nev / er is /

astray. /   **c** Iambic Hexameter line

Now that the technical terms have been defined, I would like for you to consider the technical forms of the most expressive (in my view) structures the masters have developed. Their artistic and communication usefulness has been proven many times. I want you to share in that joy.

Let me remind you that poetry uses *all* the most compressed and powerful sound effects, rules for putting words together, figures of speech, and basic principles we have discussed for prose. Ezra Pound wrote: "Go in fear of abstractions." If you can write a poem using only touch/feel/see/hear/smell words, chances are you will write most effectively.

Although working out the feet stresses and line numbers and rhyme endings is confusing at first; if you will stick with it, . . . it will become "second nature" and you will find one of the greatest life gifts in writing structured verse. Note in the Spenserian stanza above, the way the variant feet changed the rhythm of those lines. They are effective in the content because their use made the flow rough to correspond with "counter winde and tyde." But use them with care. Don't allow them to be a "cop-out" on finding the "right words" to keep the rhythm intact when that is best. *Only* use variant feet when their usage enhances content!

Writing structured poetry demands discipline . . . but oh! the dividends when that privilege is yours! Work at it with care until you truly "master the instrument." It will bring you . . . and your loved ones . . . lifetime pleasure.

THE MAJOR FORMS OF STRUCTURED POETRY

1. Blank Verse.

Any number of lines you choose of UNRHYMED Iambic (u /) Pentameter (five-foot line).

EXAMPLE:

"Is this the region, this the soil, the clime,"
Said then the lost archangel, "This the seat
That we must change for heaven this mournful gloom
For that celestial light? Be it so, since he
Who now is sovereign can dispose and bid
Whom reason hath equaled, force hath made supreme
Above his equals."

—From *Paradise Lost*
By John Milton

2. English Sonnet.

Fourteen lines of Iambic (u /) Pentameter (five-foot line) with the rhyme pattern: ababcdcdefefgg.

EXAMPLE:

That time/of year/thou mayst in me/behold   a
When yellow leaves, or none, or few, do hang   b
Upon those boughs which shake against the cold   a
Bare ruin'd choirs, where late the sweet birds sang.   b

In me thou see'st the twilight of such day   c
As after sunset fadeth in the west,   d
Which by and by black night doth take away,   c
Death's second self, that seals up all in rest.   d
In me thou see'st the glowing of such fire,   e
That on the ashes of his youth doth lie,   f
As the death-bed whereon it must expire,   e
Consum'd with that which it was nourish'd by.   f
This thou perceiv'st, which makes thy love more strong g
To love that well which thou must leave ere long.   g

—Shakespeare

3. Italian Sonnet.

Fourteen lines of Iambic (u /) Pentameter (five-foot line) with the rhyme pattern: abbaabbacdecde. Variation is allowed in the cde rhymes.

EXAMPLE:

          u /   u /   u /   u /   u /
O friend! I know not which way I must look   a
For comfort, being, as I am, opprest,   b
To think that now our life is only drest   b
For show, mean handiwork of craftsman, cook,   a
Or groom! We must run glittering like a brook   a
In the open sunshine, or we are unblest;   b
No grandeur now in nature or in book   b
Delights us. Rapine, avarice, expense,   a
This is idolatry; and these we adore: c
Plain living and high thinking are no more: c
The homely beauty of the good old cause   d
Is gone; our peace, our fearful innocence,   d
And pure religion breathing household laws.   d

—Wordsworth

4. The Folk Ballad.

Any number of stanzas. The standard ballad stanza consists of alternating lines of Iambic (u /) Tetrameter (four-foot line) and

Iambic (u /) Trimeter (three-foot line) with the rhyme scheme of abcb.

Other characteristics are: (1) it tells a story; (2) it begins close to the climax and then uses flashbacks; (3) dialogue is used as in most stories; (4) storyteller is objective; (5) simple language; (6) erratic in movement, the story is told by leaps and bounds.

EXAMPLE:

> u / u / u / u /
> The king sits in Dunfermline toune   a
>   Drinking the blude-reid wine: b
> "O whar will I get guid sailor,   c
>   To sail this schip of mine?"   b
>
> Up and spak an eldern knight,
>   Sat at the king's richt kne:
> "Sir Patrick Spens is the best sailor
>   That sails upon the se."
>
> The king has written a braid letter,
>   And signd it wi his hand,
> And sent it to Sir Patrick Spens
>   Was walking on the sand.
>
> The first line that Sir Patrick red,
>   A loud lauch lauchèd he;
> The next line that Sir Patrick red,
>   The teir blinded his ee.
>
> "O wha is this has don this deid,
>   This ill deid don to me,
> To send me out this time o' the yeir,
>   To sail upon the se?
>
> "Mak hast, mak hast, my mirry men all,
>   Our guid schip sails the morne,"
> "O say na sae, my master deir,
>   For I feir a deadlie storme.
>
> "Late, late yestreen I saw the new moone,
>   Wi the auld moone in hir arme,

And I feir, I feir, my deir master,
　　That we will cum to harme."

O our Scots nobles wer rich laith
　　To weet their cock-heild schoone;
But lang owre a' the play were playd,
　　Their hats they swam aboone.

O lang, lang may their ladies sit
　　Wi their fans into their hand,
Or eir they se Sir Patrick Spens
　　Cum sailing to the land.

O lang, lang may the ladies stand,
　　Wi their gold kems in their hair,
Waiting for thair ain deir lords,
　　For they'll se thame na mair.

Haf owre, haf owre to Aberdour,
　　It's fiftie fadom deip;
And thar lies guid Sir Patrick Spens,
　　Wi the Scots lords at his feit.

Unknown

5. The Elegy.

Any metrical pattern; any rhyme scheme; any line length. Only
requirement: a lamentation for the dead.

EXAMPLE:

In the village churchyard she lies,
Dust is in her beautiful eyes,
　　No more she breathes, nor feels, nor stirs;
At her feet and at her head
Lies a slave to attend the dead,
　　But their dust is white as hers.

Was she, a lady of high degree,
So much in love with the vanity
　　And foolish pomp of this world of ours?
Or was it Christian charity,

And lowliness and humility,
  The richest and rarest of all dowers?

Who shall tell us? No one speaks,
No color shoots into those cheeks,
  Either of anger or of pride,
At the rude question we have asked;
Nor will the mystery be unmasked
  By those who are sleeping at her side.

Hereafter?—And do you think to look
On the terrible pages of that Book
  To find her failings, faults, and errors?
Ah, you will then have other cares,
In your own shortcomings and despairs,
  In your own secret sins and terrors!

—Longfellow

6. The Dramatic Poem.

Any metrical pattern; any rhyme scheme; any line length.

Characteristics: (a) It is written by the character himself or one of the characters in the story; (b) it may be soliloquy or dialogue.

EXAMPLES: See Robert Browning's dramatic poems. Some of his most significant are *Fra Lippo Lippi, Soliloquy of the Spanish Cloister,* and *Andrea Del Sarto.*

7. The Haiku.

This beautiful structure of Japanese poetry is discussed in the chapter on compression.

8. The Tanka.

The Tanka is called by some a "capped Haiku." The first three lines compose a Haiku. This is followed by two lines of seven syllables, each of which serve only to extend the image of the Haiku, to illuminate it. No new ideas may be introduced.

EXAMPLE:

> Come and gone the season,
> Of spring, yet I have no love
> My silk dress is warm with tears.
> Like silkworm coiled in cocoon
> My heart is covered in darkness.

9. The Cinquain.

The Cinquain is based on the Japanese Haiku. Like the Tanka, it is composed of five lines, but its syllable count is 2-4-6-8-2 for a total of twenty-two syllables.

EXAMPLE:

> Why do
> You Now create
> Gossip about her? For that
> She is beautiful, wonderful,
> Therefore.

10. The Villanelle.

We have considered English and Japanese forms. Now we turn to French forms. In these, the metrical pattern and line length are the writer's option.

The Villanelle is a French form of nineteen lines. The first line is repeated in lines six, twelve, and eighteen. The third line (which rhymes with the first line) is repeated in lines nine, fifteen, and nineteen. The lines remaining may (1) all rhyme with lines one and three or (2) all use a second rhyme.

VILLANELLE

> A dainty thing's the Villanelle.
>   Sly, musical, a jewel in rhyme.
> It serves its purpose passing well.
>
> A double-clappered silver bell
>   That must be made to clink in chime,
> A dainty thing's the Villanelle;

And if you wish to flute a spell,
   Or ask a metting 'neath the lime,
It serves its purpose passing well.

You must not ask of it to swell
   Of organs grandiose and sublime—
A dainty thing's the Villanelle;

And, filled with sweetness, as a shell
   Is filled with sound, and launched in time,
It serves its purpose passing well.

Still fair to see and good to smell
   As in the quaintness of its prime,
A dainty thing's the Villanelle,
It serves its purpose passing well.

              —William Ernest Henley

11. The Rondeau.

A French form of thirteen lines with only two rhymes. The first part of the first line becomes a refrain repeated without rhyme after the eighth line and at the end of the poem. The rhyme scheme is aabbaab (refrain) aabba (refrain).

EXAMPLE:

I thank you, Love, when I behold
The splendor of the marigold;
Its brightness sets the world aglow
As does your smile. Ah! This I know
You give me wonders manifold.

You are my strength when storms are bold.
You are my warmth when winds blow cold.
You are my spring in blowing snow.
I thank you, Love.

You are my friend with hand to hold;
You are my lover to enfold
With passion I shall ne'er outgrow;
You are my teacher to bestow

Guidance wise as my map unfolds.
I thank you, Love.

12. The Triolet.

An eight-line-stanza French form where the first, fourth, and seventh lines are identical and the second and eighth are identical. There are only two final rhyming sounds.

EXAMPLE:

PREMONITION

The sun shines today.
   Will it so shine tomorrow?
Golden-bright as in May,
   The sun shines today.
Will its warm glow give way
   To a stormcloud of sorrow?
The sun shines today,—
   Will it so shine tomorrow?

13. The Roundel.

A French structure of nine lines with a refrain after the third and ninth lines. The rhyme pattern is aba (refrain) bab aba (refrain).

EXAMPLE:

Fly, white butterflies, out to sea,
Frail pale wings for the winds to try,
Small white wings that we scarce can see
   Fly.

Here and there may a chance-caught eye
Note in a score of you twain or three
Brighter or darker of tinge or dye.

Some fly light as a laugh of glee,
Some fly soft as a low long sigh;
All to the haven where each would be,
   Fly.

            —Algernon Swinburne

14. The Rondel.

This French form has fourteen lines. The first two lines are repeated as the seventh and eighth and again as the thirteenth and the fourteenth. Letting capitals stand for the repeated lines, the rhyme pattern is ABba abAB abbaAB.

EXAMPLE:

> My dreams all come true
> When you sing your life-song;
> In the world's teeming throng
> I find my joy in you.
>
> I find skies azure blue
> When you take me along;
> My dreams all come true
> When you sing your life-song.
>
> So long as we are two
> We can be brave and strong
> Our love makes us belong
> No matter where or who!
> My dreams all come true
> When you sing your life-song.

15. The Acrostic.

This is a poem in which the beginning letters of the individual lines spell out a word or words, usually related to the subject matter of the poem.

EXAMPLE:

> M arble, weep, for thou dost cover
> A dead beauty underneath thee.
> R ich, as nature could bequeath thee:
> G rant then, no rude hand remove her.
> A ll the gazers on the skies
> R ead not in fair heaven's story,
> E xpresser truth, or truer glory,
> T han they might in her bright eyes.
>
> R are, as wonder, was her wit;
> A nd like nectar ever flowing:

T ill time, strong by her bestowing
C onquered hath both life and it.
L ife, whose grief was out of fashion,
I n these times. Few so have rued
F ate, in a brother. To conclude,
F or wit, feature, and true passion.
E arth, thou hast not such another.

—Ben Jonson
On the death of a girl
Who died in 1599
At the age of twenty-four.

THE BOOK

To motivate yourself to the *hard work* of learning to write structured verse, think of a topic on which you would like to create a book of poetry . . . or think of a person to whom you would like to give a special love gift! That done, take each form, here presented, and create a poem by its rules . . . a poem whose content is personally, uniquely chosen for the book goal. When you finish the task, take it to a bindery, have it bound, and keep it for self-inspiration . . . or give it as a love gift to someone *important!*

I required this of my students who took a college course in poetry. Since the course was offered in the fall, it was completed just prior to Christmas. Parents, lovers, roommates, pastors, even poetry professors received cherished gifts from the work of that class.

Others wrote each poem toward a self-goal. One girl wrote about life dreams; a boy wrote meditations on the God/man relationship; a girl wrote her ideals of womanhood. These self-gift books were of equal value to *their* recipients.

Is there an area of your life you would like to explore in many dimensions? If so, write a poem of each structure type discussed . . . and believe me! you will gain viewpoints never possible before!

Is there someone to whom you would like to write your feelings? If so, here are different, delightful, uniquely beautiful ways of saying: "I love you" or "Thank you for caring!" or "Share a dream with me. . . ." Graduation . . . Wedding . . . Anniversary . . . Birthday . . . Thanksgiving . . . Christmas . . . Valentine's Day . . . whatever event you want to celebrate . . . whatever special message you want to communicate . . . THIS BOOK will do it for you!

Poetry is an inimitable form of expression.

Shelley said: "Poetry lifts the veil from the hidden beauty of the world, and makes familiar objects be as if they were not familiar."

Simonides said: "Poetry is a speaking picture. . . . No definition will be of any service to the person who has not really experienced poetry, and the person who has experienced it will not require a definition."

Make it yours.

19

THE WRITING OF FREE VERSE

Free verse is defined in its title. It is verse (in all senses of the imagistic, sensorial, sound-effects-oriented meaning of that term) that is free of the restraints of meter, rhyme, or stanza shape. In free verse, the poet arranges his sounds, constructs his lines, and shapes his stanzas to meet the particular needs of his poem: the subject; his emotions; his unique expression.

It is *not* an easier form than the structured styles . . . if done with earnestness and care. It *has* its own peculiar charms and strengths.

When writing free verse, you should check your balance of the following characteristics:

Compression . . . Enough? Too much?
Vivid Imagery
Most impressive format on page
Internal rhyme
Punctuation
Simile, Metaphor
Other Figures of Speech: Personification, Apostrophe, Metonymy, Synecdoche, Oxymoron, Litotes, Hyperbole, Epithet, Antithesis, Inversion

Line Break
Rhythm/Movement
Stanza Break
Detail . . . Enough? Too much?
Sentence construction effective?
Sound effects: Alliteration, Assonance, Consonance, Onomat-
    opoeia, Euphony, Cacophony
Logic
Continuity
Repetition
Symbols

That "check sheet" will keep you reminded of the important
tools available for use in free verse. Don't allow yourself to be
"slapdash" and use only the first techniques *or* words that come
to mind. Make your free verse *vital!*

The most subjective form of poetic writing, free verse demands
a knowledge of the rhythms of formal structure to be at its best.
The discipline of the other forms will give you a foundation of
rhyme/rhythm consciousness that is necessary for the clearest
communication in free verse. It cannot be given to you in rules. It
must be internalized from the formal structures and then, on
that solid foundation, free verse can wing "free" with its most impressive meanings.

Do let your imagination wing free!

When I was a college freshman, I sat alone in a classroom after
all the other students had left and wrote:

> IloveBillandIwanttobehiswife.
> There.
> I said it . . .
>   Life will
>   Never be
>   The same.

In a more recent time I wrote:

I'm like
A puppet
On a string:

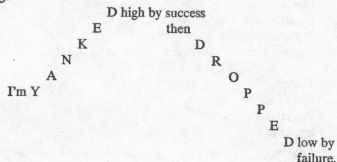

D high by success
            then
          E
       K   D
     N   R
   A   O
I'm Y   P
                              P
                            E
                              D low by
                                failure.

Lord,
Stabilize
My Center
So I may
Live
From the
Inside-Out-Steady-No-Matter-Who-Yanks-My-Strings!

Study books of free verse. Ponder various styles. Then set about developing your own.

Free verse, of course, communications any topic. I have found it uniquely expressive for prayer. So have many others. I recommend your perusal of such books as Bob Benson's *Laughter in the Walls,* Sallie Chesham's beautiful *Walking with the Wind,* and *Decision* magazine's compilation of free-verse-prayer-poems, *God, I Like You!*

There is a special beauty, poignancy, expressiveness in using this form for God conversations. Develop it for yourself. It will give you opportunity for rare heart-sharing such as this:

I'm hurt!
Quivering in heart-pain . . .
                                And You
                                Almighty God
                                You care, don't You?
You
The Sovereign of the Universe
See me
Huddled here
Like a desawdusted doll
                        Dejected
                        Deflated
                        Defeated
                                And You
                                Care!
                                Oh!
                                Thank You!

20

THE WRITING OF GREETING CARDS

It's always fun to express positive emotions about life and the people who make it so rich and beautiful and that is available in the writing of greeting cards. It may be done for money . . . there is a prolific market wide-open . . . but it is also the greatest joy to create your own . . . for your own!

Some of my former students regularly send me self-created cards. These are the ones I cherish most . . . because each word, art-form line-design has that *personal* touch! I invite you to consider this area of writing . . . professionally . . . and as sensitive expression to the people who *matter* in your life.

How do you begin?

First, study the structure of greeting cards. Note their metrical patterns and rhyme schemes. Be careful to keep the metrical patterns consistent. Although, in formally structured writing, you can write an Iambic line in which a Trochee or an Amphimacer is contained . . . it is best *not* to attempt that in this market. Note how, in professional cards, the verses run smoothly and the word inflections are always exactly as they are in normal conversation.

The ideas for greeting cards are as bountiful as human emotions. When you keep your eyes, ears, and heart open, you'll find inspiration everywhere. My son said that the following verse grew out of a term-paper assignment he had avoided until the last minute. He sat finally at the typewriter, rolled in the paper . . . and wrote:

My mind is blank; I don't know what to do;
I guess, dear Mom, you know the feeling too.
I've seen you look at me in such despair
That I would ever learn to comb my hair
Pick up my clothes, or stand up straight like you.

Your mind was blank; you didn't know what to do;
But you persisted with swats and lectures too!
You showed me: when the mind is blank, go to work
Take control of life; and never, never shirk!
And so I will . . . but first, I'll say: I love you!

I don't know how his term paper turned out, but the bit of rough verse it inspired is a treasure in the scrapbook of his mother.

The Acrostic poetic form, discussed in the chapter on poetry, is invaluable in personal greeting cards. Every person's name is special and thus the acrostic can be doubly impressive.

Greeting cards can be personally made with construction paper, scissors, paste, and felt-point pens. Magazine pictures or original art work illustrate.

Especially fancy cards can be made with the cover done in your own needlepoint. One of my friends made a needlepoint "frame" for an original picture on a greeting card to my husband. Another made a needlepoint acrostic on my recent birthday.

One of my students has done a needlepoint acrostic of each of her children which she has framed for their rooms. In one corner, she has "needleworked" a frame for a baby picture of each child. (Among the names are Matthew and Bartholomew. She said she had learned to truly appreciate names like Tom and Sam!)

Of especial beauty in personal life, this form of writing may be done professionally. To develop this outlet, work hard on compression. Selling anything longer than eight liners is rare.

If you do art work, send your card to an editor as you envision it. If accepted, it will be a more complete achievement. If not, they may buy the verse anyway.

THE WRITING OF THE AS-TOLD-TO STORY

This is an exciting type of writing because it broadens your horizons in many ways. First, you make a close friend; second, you truly *experience* in your emotions another's heartbeat and unique life venture; third, you look at the world through a totally different pair of eyes.

There are so many terrific stories in the world that *should* be told . . . and so few people who know well how to tell a story! That is how this genre developed. And what a great contribution it has been. David Wilkerson told his story to professional writers who made an impact on the world with *The Cross and the Switchblade.* These same writers achieved another internal phenomenon in *The Hiding Place,* their as-told-to story of the wonderful Corrie ten Boom.

When you know someone or read of someone who has a terrific story to tell, this is your opportunity for a rewarding personal adventure . . . as well as the chance to profoundly influence others by the storytelling. Using this device with older family members can make your "family tree" a viable, vital record for your children as you compile as-told-to accounts for personal history.

The whole key to writing the as-told-to story is to literally "get inside" the skin of the protagonist. You have to listen and listen to their tapes or to them personally . . . until you feel "inside" their spirit . . . living, reacting, feeling as they did in the experience.

It is possible to write the as-told-to from the person's written efforts. This is usually unsatisfactory because the average person simply does not go into enough detail so that you can begin to "get inside." When I was doing a weekly series of this type of story for a magazine, I was often assigned someone who had written out the story. I always tried to augment this, at least, with a telephone call. Hearing the person's voice adds insight. Pictures are almost an imperative.

Tapes between you and the storyteller can be most helpful. Through questioning and probing, listening carefully to vocal intonations and shading, you ultimately can arrive at a genuine "heart-feel."

Of course, the best way is personal interview. If you can be with the person in hours of dialogical conversation where you can *see* facial expressions, observe twisting hands, see agitated movement when memories become too painful to bear in one position . . . where you can ask questions probing the inner regions of the spirit . . . then you are best equipped to go to the typewriter and pour out the story truly from the "heartbeat" of the other person.

This type of story is always written first person. It is striving for the immediacy, intimacy, and specificity of personal sharing even though it may be concerned with a broader issue. Wilkerson's story shocked the church arena about their appalling apathy and ignorance of youth problems. But had it been written as a general exposé, its readership would have been very small. Written with the power of the first-person account, it rocked the world.

You can find your subject by understanding the dimension of a person's story . . . or you may find it by your concern about a problem that can best be presented to the reader by allowing him to *participate* in the confusion as lived by someone. Beth Day had that desire in regard to a general exposé of hospitals. Through a lot of footwork and interviewing, she finally found a person whose story would personalize the problem so that the readership would be wide and the impact of the problem vivid. The result was her book *I'm Done Crying!*

One of my students, a Minister of Youth, who wanted his church to understand the need for funding a summer camp program, wrote a series of as-told-to stories from youth whose lives had changed because of the camp program. The author put the series on dittos; bound them inexpensively with heavy stock and ring binders; distributed them to the church membership. When the budgeting was allocated, he received $3,000 more than asked.

One of my colleagues at the university traversed the nation each summer looking up people on her family tree. Taping every conversation, making prolific notes, visiting every possible historical spot, she made her winter-time hobby the writing of as-told-to stories of the people who formed the background of her own life. She keeps these in a ring binder that ever grows thicker . . . and her family background becomes ever-more fascinating to her, to her current family and friends, to generations to come.

There is no limit to the writing potential of this genre. I invite you to join in the exciting adventure.

22

THE WRITING OF FICTION

Mark Twain wrote, in a letter to William Dean Howells, this account:

> Speaking of the ill luck of starting a piece of literary work wrong—and again and again; always aware that there is a way, if you could think it out, which would make the thing slide effortlessly from the pen—the one right way, the sole form for YOU, the other forms being for men whose lines those forms are, or who are capabler than yourself. . . . Last summer I started sixteen things wrong—three books, thirteen magazine articles—and could only make two little wee things, 1,550 words altogether succeed—only that out of piles and stacks of diligently wrought MS., the labor of six weeks' unremitting effort. I could make all of those things go if I would take the trouble to begin each one half a dozen times on a new plan. But none of them was important enough except one. . . .
>
> A week ago I examined the MS.—10,000 words—and saw that the plan was a totally impossible one—for me; but a new plan suggested itself, and straightway the tale began to slide from the pen with ease and confidence. I think I've struck the right one this time. I have already put 12,000 words of it on paper. . . . In the present form I could spin

sixteen books out of it with comfort and joy; but I shall deny myself and restrict it to one.

But, as we discover in his later letters, he guessed wrong. This new play did not work either. He reports that he wasted numberless hours on the piece and finally gave it up for a bad effort and threw it away.

I find it encouraging to know that even the great masters of writing creatively had such problems . . . don't you? But . . . there is a way that will help both the masters . . . and the to-be masters like you . . . to avoid such waste of time and effort. Let's consider some basic rules of good organization.

1. Keep your Journal daily.

2. Record and work in your Notebook regularly.

3. Become an intent newspaper reader and clipper.

You would be surprised to know how heavily professional writers in fiction of all genre—short story, novel, drama, movie—rely upon the newspaper for ideas. Here is daily reportage of humanity in action: the personalities from which good stories come, . . . events that stimulate ideas for original plots . . . complications "stranger than fiction" could ever be!

4. Get another shoe box (boxes) and begin a file for the writing of fiction!

A suggested group of files that will begin your work in fiction and into which you will place your clippings from newspapers, notes, and other mind-stimulators is this.

CHARACTERS	SETTINGS
Boy children	Homes
Girl children	Colleges
Group children	Boarding schools
Young men	Professional businesses
Young women	Blue-collar businesses
Young couples	City
Mature men	Country
Mature women	Foreign
Mature couples	Rooms for personalities
Aged men	Rivers
Aged women	Recreational spots
Aged couples	Dining places
Animals	Travel settings

COMPLICATIONS OF LIFE	COMPLICATION SOLUTIONS
Tragic	Violent
Comic	Ingenius
Extraordinary	Love or acts of the Spirit

Please understand these are only suggestions . . . and only beginnings. You will continue to have more and more specific files as you understand the kinds of people and complications of life and themes in which you are personally interested.

5. Cross-index materials in your files.

Your files are valuable simply because of classified material in general headings. But they become more valuable if you will spend time going through files and jotting down your ideas that jell together in diverse files. Each story will contain characters, settings, complications, and a solution.

Cross-indexing is a vital memoranda to giving your files their greatest possible value.

6. When you have free time, write character sketches of personalities, descriptions of settings, run-throughs of complication outlines, et cetera.

This kind of writing gives you practice that is essential; it also gives you varied full-fledged ways of looking at the contents of your files that will stimulate your mind to full-blown excitement when you are prepared to write the story.

7. Set up a picture file.

This file may have exactly the same headings as your content file. Harry Mark Petrakis, in *Stelmark: A Family Recollection,* wrote of exercises he did with files: "Using photographs of men and women, country and city scenes, I'd begin by describing each photo in a paragraph of prose. I'd keep paragraph and photo in a folder. From time to time, I'd select one of the folders and rework that particular paragraph, expanding the visual description and introducing smells and sounds not visible in the photo but inherent in the scene. I'd also try to create an aura of the mood the scene suggested to me, whether of sadness or of joy."

Petrakis sets up the ideal use of picture files for exercise. An additional use is to give you, the writer, the specific nuances of color, dimension, and quantity in landscape or city scenes . . . eye color, facial expression, or body stance with people. The study of pictures is always advantageous to precise description.

8. Solicit help.

If you have parents, siblings, or friends who have time to do more extensive reading than you . . . or would be willing to make files for you from collected sources . . . ask their help.

THE DEVELOPMENT OF CHARACTERS

There are two genre of characters you will use in your stories: (1) the stereotype and (2) the personality. In the stereotype, you will picture persons with general characteristics of four basic types: (a) the nationality: typical Englishman, Italian, or German; (b) the occupational: lawyer, rancher, or plumber; (c) the socialite: typical blind date, old-maid aunt, or member of the Jet Set; (d) the typical character: the Gambler, the Prude, the Prejudiced, the Worry Wart. In this genre, your people will be unrolled in line with the reader's general stereotyped opinion. But, in development of the personality, you will unroll a character so that he is unique in every sense. He is an *individual*. He is more than an Irishman, a policeman, a typical weekend guest, or a Happy-Go-Lucky. He is a *peculiar self*.

The first genre is easy to depict and work with.

The second is difficult . . . and the essential element to good story writing. So how does one go about developing personalities?

Here is a suggested format.

* Get a picture of your personality.

Go through your files and other sources until you can look at a picture and say: "Ah yes! There *is* Jeb Langer!" Place his picture in a place where you can study it in moments when your hands are busy with other things: over the kitchen sink, in the side of your mirror, and so on. Spend time with it, with pencil in your hand, striving to detail all of the aspects of personality that come to you.

For help in description of young attractive people, a good source is your Sears catalog. The same model may be used as many as a dozen times in various poses and moods in the same issue. Through the years, the same models are often used. I have files on several, each of which probably shows the same person, through the years, in forty or fifty different stances, outfits, and facial expressions. This can be helpful in exploring personality for description and varied reactions.

But for real character study, you will need to go to magazines to find people who are angry, frightened, in rural settings, in lush elegant settings, et cetera. And when you find your personality, you will begin to learn of him or her in ways that could not have been that specific before.

I remember an author who spoke in a graduate seminar and said she could never remember the color of her character's eyes until she finally hit on the use of pictures. There, she had before her *that person* and it was easy for her to write out all the specifics so that she *knew* that person as if he lived next door.

* Study that picture and write and write and write about your personality. Begin with his birth; describe his parents; his siblings; the socioeconomic level of his home; the educational level in which he grew up; specific experiences of his life from birth all the way through to the age at which you want to begin your story. This will give you a background knowledge of this personality you can gain no other way.

But there is more.

Not only do you understand the personality as writer . . . but you can draw on all of that information in your story. In one of my short stories, for example, I wanted to describe the fear that was dissipating the happiness of my protagonist. Julie had just been elected head cheerleader. Her friends were exuberant, but Julie walked away from the noisy group to stand alone. She tried to analyze her emotions . . . and then she remembered. . . .

It had been like this when she went to Coney Island with Daddy. It had been a glorious day and, on the way home, they sang, one song after another, and their voices seemed to grow stronger and truer as they sang. By the time they reached the high rise where Julie lived with her mother, they were so filled with the communion of their shared feelings that they were beyond words. They rode the elevator to the apartment soundlessly, almost motionlessly, as if the contentment between them were something so precious it might be shattered by a breath.

As they walked down the hall, Julie had cupped her palms about the day as if to preserve its quicksilver beauty forever. When they opened the door, the immediate vision of Mother's angry face shattered the ecstasy. Julie could almost see the mood spurt apart like a dissolving soap bubble. Mother screamed and raged as if resolved to destroy the intangible radiance between them. She seemed to believe that by lunging against their love, she could stamp it out.

Perhaps one always had to pay for joy. Perhaps for every love-lined day would come a pain-ripping night. Perhaps every minute of laughter exacted a year of tears. Perhaps happiness was not worth its price.

Only through such thorough understanding of your personalities can you provide true motivation for their behavior and human relations in your story. A particularly good book you might peruse on the psychology of motivation is *Discovering Ourselves* by Edward Strecker. The ways our culture unconsciously conditions the nonverbal ways we communicate is analyzed in *The Silent Language* by Edward Hall and would make valuable reading. I also recommend *Mirror for Man* by Clyde Kluckhohn which discusses race, personality, language, and customs. Margaret Mead called it "the best contemporary introduction to modern anthropology." Another reference book you might like to consider is the Dictionary of Fictional Characters compiled by William Freeman. More than twenty thousand characters created in novels, short stories, poems, plays, and operas are delineated here and can be mind stimulating.

There are three basic ways of establishing personalities in fiction: (1) what the character says; (2) what the character does; (3) what the author tells the reader about the character. The less reliance on the latter, the more objective is the writer; the more reliance, the more subjective his story.

There have been nine devices specifically developed for such personality establishment. Let's consider them.

Nine Ways of Presenting Personality:

1. Physical Appearance.

This will come with your work with pictures. Strive, in such description, to be as succinct as possible, relying on the "peculiar characteristics" of the person's appearance: the wart on the nose, the dimple in the chin, the unusually hairy hands.

2. Movements, Gestures, Mannerisms, and Habits.

This will evolve from your background study of the culture and atmosphere of the personality's life. Edward Hall's book will be excellent stimulus here; also Susanne Langer's *Philosophy in a New Key: A Study in the Symbolism of Reason, Rite, and Art* is a good reference book of ideas of body language, sacrament, myth, abstraction, et cetera.

Detail these in your background writing. You can often *show* your personality's reaction through a peculiar gesture developed in childhood. The reader will not need to be *told* the emotions current; he will know because the gesture stems from those same emotions lived in other situations.

Pictures of Notebook entries of these characteristics of people will be helpful. Sir Laurence Olivier has described this process in an interview with Kenneth Harris which was printed in the *Observer*, March 2, 1969:

> I sometimes, on the top of a bus, see a man. I begin to won-
> der about him. I see him do something, make a gesture. Why
> does he do it like that? Because he must be like THIS. And
> if he is like this, he would do—in a certain situation—that.
> Sometimes, months later, when I am thinking about a bit of
> business [the actor's term for movements, gestures, manner-
> isms on stage], I hit on a gesture or movement or a look
> which I feel instinctively is right. Perhaps not till later, per-
> haps a week after I have been making that gesture, I realize
> where it came from—the man on the top of the bus. Then I
> realize that the gesture looks right because it WAS right and
> it was right because it was real.

The same kind of observation of real life will make these tools "right" for the writer in presenting personality as surely as they do the actor on stage.

Christopher Isherwood, in *A Berlin Diary*, wrote, "I am a cam-era with its shutter open, quite passive, recording not thinking. Recording the man shaving at the window opposite and the woman in the kimono washing her hair. Someday all this will have to be developed, carefully fixed, printed." The daily observation and study of PEOPLE THEMSELVES cannot be overemphasized. One author said that whenever she stepped on a plane where she would have undisturbed time to observe a kaleidoscope of humanity, she would whisper: "For what I am about to receive, O Lord, I am truly thankful!"

3. Behavior Toward Others.

This is another device of showing instead of telling. A person who ignores social courtesies is revealing truths about himself. A person who eats alone, a person who is always in the midst of people laughing and talking, a person who seems unaware of others' presence are all showing us, in their behavior, aspects of their personalities.

4. Speech.

A fundamental rule is that each character delineates personality with a unique rhythm, locution, idiosyncrasy, brevity or long-windedness, syntactical structure, and word selection. This is surely one of the most difficult devices to conquer.

There are two basic rules: (a) Condense. Strive to have your personality say in forty words what he would take four hundred for in real life; (b) never write dialogue for its own sake; each sentence should either portray personality or advance plot. Study the style of the masters. I especially recommend John O'Hara who could, in a single line, tell a personality's social standing, education, approach to life, ambitions, and frustrations. And as the reader "hears" him utter that line, he makes his own decision concerning the personality's strengths and weaknesses.

Slang should be held to a minimum. However it is an effective tool if used well . . . and cautiously. A slang dictionary may be helpful in working with a personality whose speech is filled with certain idioms, colloquialisms and jargon available in our language. One of the best is American Thesaurus of Slang by Lester Berrey and Melvin Van Den Bark. The first portion of the book deals with general slang and colloquialisms. The second consists of specialized speech such as the underworld; military; entertainment; regionalisms, campus, and so on. There is also a section on the origins and dates of the slang expressions which is helpful.

Less comprehensive and less expensive is a book called Dictionary of American Slang edited by Harold Wentworth and

Stuart Berg Flexner. Available in paperback, it has more than eight thousand alphabetized entries with dates of usage and actual quotations given from the language of the "beat" generation, hobos, Madison Avenue promotors, et cetera.

Dialects are excellent in portraying character, but they require a great deal of work for the writer. Many writers simply ignore dialect because of this, but to be at your best, you should understand the manner as much as the content of a personality's speech.

The two best books to assist you in utilizing dialect are Manual of Foreign Dialects and Manual of American Dialects, by Lewis and Marguerite Herman (published by Prentice-Hall). But to bring dialect to a personality with perfection is an arduous task.

A working compromise that many writers use is a mimimum amount of dialect. Some examples: dropping the "h" in all words in cockney; substituting "d" and "t" for "th" in German; substituting "y" for "j" in Swedish; the aspirate "uh" ending to final consonants in Italian.

Another helpful source may be found in your library's files of the magazines *American Speech* and *Dialect Notes*. Here you may find classified lists of idiomatic expressions, region by region, with many treatises on the manner of pronunciation. Catherine Marshall wrote that when she was writing her novel *Christy,* she spent a great deal of time reading actual transcripts of court trials in cases of mountain feuding. This gave her authentic idioms, pronunciations, and jargon. When dialect is essential to your story, there are places where the necessary study can be done. But it *is* work.

You can help yourself, beginning now, by training your ear to listen carefully to foreign-speaking people as well as American-dialect speakers and recording in your Notebook their oddities of expression.

Some of the major problems in writing dialogue are (1) Striving to be too bright! Even though we decry the trite simile or the hackneyed in writing . . . we still speak it! Try to keep dialogue as it truly is in life. Most personalities do not utter profundities of wit or wisdom at the "flip of a lip." (2) Striving too hard to achieve an idiom so that the personality gets bogged down in jargon.

5. Attitude Toward Self.

Is self-love present? Self-esteem? To use Thomas Harris' book title, is the attitude toward self: "I'm OK; You're OK" . . . or is it the frequent attitude: "You're OK; I'm not OK"? *Show* that attitude in the actions, thoughts, and speech of your personality, and vital insights into the character are thus revealed. Again, the person's background is vital for your expertise in understanding and portraying this attitude.

6. Attitude of Others Toward the Character.

Is the person treated with respect . . . pity . . . equality . . . rejection . . . diffidence . . . hostility by others in the story? The *showing* of mannerisms and speech to delineate prevailing and personal attitudes is an important device.

7. Physical Surroundings.

I had a professor who used to say: "If I can spend an hour in your room, I can tell you all about yourself." Although this is probably an exaggeration, it isn't by much. You could simply walk through my house and know immediately much about me: my love of books, my love of records, my love of music, the people I love the most—all of this by a casual glance at the filled bookcases, filled record cabinets, musical instruments, personally chosen photographs . . .

Develop this essential part of the character with the same kind of detail you do his or her personality. Have pictures, maps, and extensive word sketches available so you can use this device in presenting personality.

8. The Past.

Although this is a specific device, we have already discussed it in understanding the personality. Only when fully developed in the writer's mind can motivation and credibility be established.

9. Simile and Metaphor.

Though this can be overdone to the point of mysticism and obscurity, it can, sometimes, be an effective device in portraying character. "He was like the Rock of Gibraltar to his children" is a simile that many people would use who knew my father. It was one we often used among ourselves and to ourselves. He was an unwavering tower of strength that we could hold on to wherever in the wide world we were. I remember calling him one time in a moment of personal distress. When he hung up the phone, my mother asked what I said. He replied: "Nothing. She just cried." And that was true. Just to let my tears flow while in the nonvisual presence of my "Rock of Gibraltar" was enough to give me the courage to go back into my battle.

When I called my brother and told him that Daddy had died, his first words were: "My Rock is gone; what shall I do?" It was the heart-cry of all of his children.

Although this device should be used with care, it is a means of portraying character succinctly, effectively, uniquely.

The major element that makes a story great is when we recognize the characters as real flesh-and-blood human beings . . . when we, in short, can *Identify* with them . . . when we can "get inside the skin" of that person and *experience* the story as that person.

In Daphne de Maurier's *Rebecca,* I literally *became* the "second wife" and simultaneously adored and feared Rebecca. I participated in the whole experience of that book because, although my life was diverse in specifics, I *understood* how it felt to be shy, awkward, unable to measure up to standards set by someone more beautiful, more talented, more graceful . . . and because those are universal emotions, I could become "the second wife" to a degree that the story is a great one to me.

Identification stems from emotion.

If your person can evoke in me, the reader, such universals as love, hate, jealousy, fear, greed, I can understand and participate with him. In Tennessee Williams' *Glass Menagerie,* Laura's wistful dreams are contagious because we all have spent hours in dreams. In the first scene of Ibsen's *Hedda Gabler,* he creates wonderful identification in the humiliation inflicted on Miss Tesman by Hedda. We have all been humiliated in life and we immediately identify with Miss Tesman and despise Hedda.

Psychologists tell us that fear is the strongest emotion of life. We are afraid of so many things.

I remember that when my father's body was lying in state, people thronged in to pay their respects . . . and to offer condolences to us children who had grown up in the shadow of this Giant. One of my brothers stayed in a small room by himself for such long periods that I would go to seek him out to greet the crowds. I went in one time and he looked at me with poignant grief in his eyes and said: "I feel like a little boy lost in the woods. I keep telling myself that Daddy will come and take me home . . . and then I remember that I'm an adult; my father is dead; he will never give me guidance, strength, or a helping hand again. His death leaves me vulnerable." I went in and sat with him, sharing in the fear that clutched our hearts as we faced a future without paternal love.

No reason or logic governs emotion. But once experienced, we never forget. And if you, the writer, can create people with universal emotions, your readers will identify . . . and this is the touchstone of good literature.

A list I once made of universal emotions is given below. It is only a one-time think-through, but it may stimulate you to form one of your own.

Humiliation	Injustice
Hunger for love	Desire for vengeance
Search for God	Loyalty
Love	Hunger for companionship
Desire for achievement	Hate

Fear . . . for life, for loved one's life . . .
Fear of rejection . . . of fire . . . of flood . . . of loss of home . . . of hatred . . . of pain . . . ad infinitum.

THE SETTING OF A WORK OF FICTION

It is said that setting may perform one of four basic roles. These are: (1) Place as character . . . where the setting affects the story as much as personalities and events within it . . . an example would be the heath in Thomas Hardy's *The Return of the Native;* (2) Place as destiny . . . where personalities are formed and enhanced or hampered by the setting . . . and there is no choice involved; (3) Place as narrative element . . . which means that the setting is utilized to develop characters, complicate plot, et cetera; (4) Place as backdrop . . . where it provides the landscape, the geographical arrangement, the atmospheric ingredients for the story.

In developing Setting, you will want to use your files as you did for Character Development. Find pictures of the countryside . . .

the important houses, campuses, churches, and other structures
. . . the important rooms. Study them until you can capture their
"feel" as well as sensory appeal.

If your story covers a specific geographical locale, you may
want to draw a map. An excellent example of this device is to be
found in the front pages of Catherine Marshall's *Christy* where
she includes the map of Cutter Gap, the locale she used in the
writing. This enables the writer to always be certain mentally
where things are located, the time it would take to get from one
place to another, whether it could be done by foot or any other
means.

You may want to keep these visual aids over your kitchen sink
or in the side slot of your mirror in order to study them even
when your hands are busy doing other things. Setting is important
in whichever role it is developed in your story.

COMPLICATIONS OF PLOT

I feel that most complications for storytelling can be placed
in two categories: (1) Conflict and (2) Search. Eudora Welty
wrote in the *Atlantic Monthly* in 1949: "On some level all
stories are stories of search. Perhaps quest is a better word. In
most stories, at any rate, someone is in quest of something. Someone is in quest of a wife, a fortune, an honor, a murderer, a vic-
tory, truth, righteousness, knowledge, power, maturity. Whenever
anyone starts in quest of anything, a story is begun."

Although I see Miss Welty's point, I still feel more comfortable
with a dual classification: (1) Conflict and (2) Search, for I believe it gives more specificity. There is usually conflict in any
search that is worthwhile, but the two seem to me to stand as separate entities.

Conflict implies opposing wills. It may occur in three ways:
(1) conflicting wills, goals, purposes of two people or groups of
people; (2) conflicting wills, goals, or purposes of several people
or groups; (3) conflicting wills, goals, or purposes within one
person.

The search is initiated out of a personality's own desires . . .
or it may be thrust upon him by another's will or by events over

which he has no control . . . or the effect of the success or failure of a search may form a story.

In your Notebook, keep a list of conflicts and searches that intrigue you. When you have time, take one and write a sketch of how such a story could be developed. Let your mind follow the principle of "What if . . ." so that your imagination can have fullest rein. Be closely observant of conflicts and searches in life about you . . . in your reading, listening, and viewing. Consistent listening will provide you with ideas when you need a "spark."

Most of your complications will flow naturally, however, as you develop specific personalities in specific settings; the resulting conflicts or searches will come to you in surprising ways.

There are basically two *points of view* from which you can write your story. Each has its own strengths and weaknesses and you must weigh one against the other. They are: (1) First Person; (2) Third Person or Omniscient.

A first-person story has many strengths. Among them are directness, immediacy of action, veracity, clarity of thought, and an intriguing simplicity. Its limitation is a restricted point of view, for you cannot go beyond knowledge that you would have in that situation. You cannot know what goes on inside the head of another person or in another location unless you are told or eavesdrop. So although strong in intimate identification, it is presenting a story through a narrow lens.

Third person or omniscience is the most versatile, flexible, and unrestricted viewpoint. Here you can make selective use of a number of person's points of view, borrowing a specific personality's vision site when it meets your goal. You can take a panoramic view of events, giving accounts of simultaneous occurrences in disparate settings. Its limitation is loss of the lure of first-person sharing; the immediate direct atmosphere of imparting a personal "slice of life."

The determination is made on the theme and background of your story. If it is basically one person's story, First Person is your strongest tool. If you are dealing with a saga that embraces a lot of life in dramatic incidents taking place hundreds of miles apart, Third Person, or Omniscience, is almost imperative.

Both are strong. Equally strong. The choice is made by your goal and tools in a particular story.

23

THE WRITING FOR CHILDREN

Although the structure of storytelling for children is the same as for adults, this is a totally different kind of writing. If you would like to speak to children, your first job should be to go to the children's room of your library and spend days there submerging yourself in what children read, the story styles and dialogue lines they respond to, and the vocabulary dimension with which they are comfortable.

The way you can tell which books to read is from the covers. Read en masse all the books that are well-worn. Those that are still new and fresh-looking, omit. Study carefully the approach of the writers whom children read prolifically.

Some fundamentals you will notice immediately are: the difference in vocabulary; children think in pictures; children are imaginative in a dimension beyond the adult, but also realistic in a dimension beyond the adult; you have to be truly honest in your writing.

Many beginning writers don't zero in on these characteristics. They erroneously assume that most children's work is fantasy. This is not true. There is a beautiful body of literature of fantasy for children . . . but it is the most difficult writing to do . . . because children are so realistic along with their ability to fantasize. So begin with that understanding. And if you must write fantasies, study the good ones carefully. *Mary Poppins, Alice in Wonderland,* and *Fog Magic* are excellent examples of classic work.

Other types of children's stories that are dearly loved are: Animal Stories (Examples: *Rabbit Hill, Bambi, Grocery Kitty*); Stories of Other Lands (Examples: *Strawberry Girl, Island on the Beam, Wings for Nikias*); and Historical Writing (Examples: *Henry's Lincoln, Treason at the Point*).

It is my opinion that the most prolific market lies in the historical category. Bobbs-Merrill, for example, has a series called "Childhoods of Young Americans." Many denominations have books written annually about children on mission fields, missionaries or other church leaders as children, historical church figures as children, or historical events as could have been perceived through the eyes of a child.

Again, this is a form of writing that can be done for personal-gift giving. The delightful LP record, *Free to be You and Me,* came into being because Marlo Thomas was trying to find a gift for her niece. Confronted with the lack of records available (like none!) dealing with self-image and life-understanding for children, Marlo Thomas created this significant recording.

The children in your life will be especially pleased if, instead of *Mary Poppins,* you give them a book of a story written by YOU . . . and, if you have that capability, illustrated by you with either pen, photos, or selected magazine pictures. You can have the book bound inexpensively at a bindery or you can put its pages in a ring notebook. Either way it is personally special and precious to the children about whom you care most!

And as you observe their reactions to your story, you will know whether or not it is publishable. Profit by the weaknesses they spot; the points where their interest lags; the times their eyes sparkle with suspense and excitement. On this "authoritative" response, you can achieve a draft of the story that you may want to send to a publisher for consideration.

Writing for children has a tingling delight to it that no other style has. For it allows the writer to go back to that wonderland and explore the world again through innocent eyes.

24

THE WRITING OF DRAMA

Drama differs from every other form of writing . . . in that it is written to appeal to the ear. All other forms of literature are written to appeal to the eye.

This fundamental difference is the one that you must bear in mind constantly when you are working on a play. You no longer have the tools of narration, exposition, or description available. You are limited to the tools of dialogue and action. And you must remember that the dialogue is to be spoken, not read. That makes a tremendous difference.

Basically, the beginning creation of a story to be performed on stage is the same as the writing of fiction. The technical steps have different names, but they are essentially part of the same process.

The specific stages of the writing of drama are these:

1. The Germinal Idea.

This is almost the same process discussed in developing complications in our discussion of fiction. Here, your files and Notebook will be vital. This is not the total concept of the play, but it is the initiating springboard of what you want to do in the story.

2. The Collection.

This, essentially, is where you begin to gather together your pictures of characters and places, write biographies of characters and understanding of the role of places. Explore the era of the drama for thoughts of costuming, dialects, sets . . . In this period, you amass the general understanding of your characters, situations, conflicts, searches, and solutions. This step is the one where your most intensive research should be done and made available to you in written form.

3. The Rough Scenario.

This is the first draft of organizing all of your work into a collective whole. It should contain the following elements:

ROUGH SCENARIO

a. Working Title (probably not the final title, but one you can live with now).
b. Conflict and/or Search.
c. Form: Identify whether you are writing tragedy, comedy, or melodrama.
d. Setting and Time of the scenes and acts of the play.
e. Theme.
f. Characters: Protagonist identified with relationships formulated with other characters.
g. Complications.
h. Story: A detailed outline from the rise of the first curtain to the fall of the last curtain.
i. Thought: Articulate the meaning of the play; the role each major character contributes to that meaning.
j. Dialogue: A statement about dialogue: use of slang, dialect, or other types of general dialogue.
k. Schedule: A personal timetable for working on the play scene by scene.

4. The Scenario.

This is the formal "treatment" of the play. This is the step toward which all others have built. This is the one that allows you to so completely structure the play that you are free, later, to focus on that all-important aspect of writing dialogue.

The elements contained in a Scenario are:

a. Title.
b. Time and Place as they will appear on script.
c. Characters: Descriptions of each.
d. Narrative: A prose narration of the play, scene by scene, concentrating on plot and story.

    e.   Working outline: A detailed outline of the play, scene by scene (be as specific as possible).

The Scenario is the final organization of your "thinking" period of creation. If you have it written in detailed specificity, you are, then, free to focus full attention on making this story live in action and dialogue on a stage.

5. The First Draft.

By this time, you should know your material thoroughly. You should understand your people, their conflicts and/or searches, and the way you plan to make resolutions. As you sit down to put it in the actual form for a play, try not to write a *great* play; simply write *your* play. Let the dialogue run freely. Use a tape recorder when it is helpful to listen to how the dialogue would sound. Be careful of monologues. Shakespeare was a great one with soliloquies, but you aren't Shakespeare yet! So try to keep more than one person on stage most of the time so that dialogue is going on rather than monologues.

With the scenario by your side, you should be able to let your mind work creatively and loosely for the hard organizing, understanding, researching part is complete. The tighter your scenario, the easier will be your first draft. The worrying is complete. Now turn yourself to the joy of allowing that story to become a concrete entity.

6. The Run-through.

If possible, when the First Draft is completed, get a group to do a Reader's Theater run-through of the play. As you listen to other people reading dialogue and envision action on the stage, you will identify problems that can be corrected.

25

THE OPEN DOORS OF PROFESSIONAL WRITING

To give you an idea of the array of open doors in writing creatively, let me briefly set up some of those which lead to excitingly unique worlds.

The Writing of Exposition

1. Fillers for Magazines. There are four types: (a) Humor; (b) Information; (c) Inspiration; (d) News. Short, succinct bits to fill up magazine pages.
2. Short Article for Magazines. 300–1,200 words; 700–800 words average.
3. The Biographical Sketch. Researched material written in third person.
4. The How-to Article. Tells "how to do" anything.
5. The Institutional Article. Information about any institution; e.g. the Crackerjack Co., United Fund, or whatever.
6. The Personal-experience Article.
7. Magazine Columns.
8. Syndicated Newspaper Column.
9. Full-length Article. Average: 2,500 words.
10. Fact Serials. Information about experiences or movements, e.g. "I worked on the Warren Commission," "The Facts About the Catholic Stand on Abortion," and others.

11. Government Writing. Turning out the millions of words that go into all the "information" books available through the Government Printing Office.
12. Curriculum Writing for Sunday School.
13. Curriculum Writing for Vacation Bible School.
14. Curriculum Writing for Church-Extended Sessions.

The Writing of Fiction

1. Short Stories.
2. Full-length Stories.
3. The Short-Short.
4. The Novelette.
5. The Novel.

The Writing of Poetry

1. Serious.
2. Light Verse.
3. Greeting-card Verse.
4. Books.

The Writing of Free Verse

1. Serious.
2. Light.
3. Photo-writing Books.
4. Small Greeting-card-type Booklets.
5. Books.

The Writing of Drama

1. The Three Act Play.
2. The One Act Play.
3. The Musical.
4. Radio Writing. (Has a specialized lingo and technique that would have to be mastered in addition.)
5. Television Writing. (Has a specialized process that would have to be mastered since story would unfold from camera

angles. Totally different format, although basic ingredients of writing drama are the same.)

6. Filmstrip Writing. (Specialized information would be needed.)
7. Moviescript Writing. (Specialized techniques would have to be mastered.)

The Writing of the As-Told-To Story

1. As-told-to first-person Article or Book.
2. Researched Third-person Biographical Article or Book.

The Writing for Children

1. Fantasy.
2. Animal Stories.
3. Life-in-Other-Lands Stories.
4. Historical.

Other Open Doors

1. Quizzes. Four types: Matching, Multiple Choice, Fill-in, Single Answer.
2. Songwriting.
3. Ghost Writing. (Similar to "as told to" except your name does not appear. Many public figures, including ministers, who have something to say but don't know *how* to say it in a way to appeal to the eye will be interested in hiring someone to set down their ideas in a readable fashion.)
4. Business Writing. (Writes reports, releases, publicity, bulletins, training manuals, sales letters, form letters, advertising, public relations, and promotion copy.)
5. Photo Writing. (Utility of slides and words to compose a created unit of presenting a philosophy or story. Or can be a book composed of photos and words complementing each other until a fusion of the two arts is achieved.)

26

THE MECHANICS OF PROFESSIONAL WRITING

1. Have a place to write.

Work out some arrangement where you may organize all of your working materials so they will be at hand when you need them. Allocate a specific room, corner, closet, table, desk as your place to write. Strive to find a place where neatness is not an essential. I have found that creation is a messy business! Not only is my desk covered with all the "stuff of writing," but there is a constant glass of Coke, a saucer with dried crumbs from last night's cake, and a stack of unironed clothes. The best writers I know have this kind of freedom. Anyone who writes on a highly polished desk with "everything in its place" is a rare individual . . . and I have yet to meet him!

2. Have a time to write.

Keep this appointment as faithfully as you would keep a job. This is a contract you make with yourself . . . and with God . . . to develop your talent as much as possible in the time you are able to set aside. Be faithful to your writing hours.

3. Organize your time.

The following schedule may help you establish priorities.
Writing: 60 per cent
Filing, marketing, et cetera: 10 per cent

Study: 10 per cent
Reading: 20 per cent

4. Use a typewriter.

Except when it isn't possible to have a typewriter with you . . .
all writing should be done on the typewriter . . . and that includes Journal and Notebook work. The reason I say that is because you need the discipline of learning to "think through your
fingers" so that you can ultimately record as quickly as you can
think. Especially for Journal and Notebook work, you will want
to write rapidly . . . letting your thoughts flow swiftly to the
paper capturing all the emotional pull of the moment. With this
as practice, you will become proficient enough to do all the typing
of your manuscripts for marketing purposes.

All manuscripts should be typed, double-spaced, with a ten-
space paragraph indentation. Many editors appreciate it—
especially if you are an unknown to them—if you will put your
name and address in the top left corner of each page. In the top
right corner, editors appreciate an estimate of word length of exposition and fiction.

Be sure to enclose with each submission a stamped, self-
addressed envelope for the return of the manuscript. If this is not
included, many magazines have a policy of throwing unsolicited
pieces away.

5. Build a list of magazines and/or book publishers for whom you would like to write. Make notations of the style of writing and the audience of each.

When you submit a piece to an editor of your choice and it is
returned, do not cry! Now that I have said that, I'll admit the reality that you will anyway and so we'll go from there!

Every piece of writing is a piece of yourself. So when a piece of
writing is rejected, you feel that a part of self has been rejected.
And this can be devastating.

What you, ultimately, have to understand is that this is not
true. You really are submitting to editors who *may* have over-
stocked on that particular type of manuscript (most rejection
slips read that way!) . . . but you have to admit that it *could* be
true.

Also you have to know that editors are human beings with particular likes and dislikes. And if one editor does not like your manuscript, it is a reflection of taste, frequently, rather than of quality. My favorite story involves a piece of exposition. I loved it (don't we always?) and sent it confidently to an editor who returned it with a personally scribbled rejection slip with a vehemently negative response. I reread the exposition (after I had cried for a proper interval!) and decided I still loved it. It said exactly what I wanted to say the way I wanted to say it. So I sent it to another editor who bought it and published it on the cover of his magazine.

Moral of the story: What is one editor's anathema is another editor's delight! It *is* true!

So. The larger your list of editors, the better your chances of publication. Try to make it a rule that a returned manuscript does not remain on your desk longer than twenty-four hours.

Always reread it after a rejection. Strive to see, objectively, if it does need revision. But, if it still states your idea the way you want to state it, *believe in it* and send it to another editor.

6. Keep manuscripts neat.

After several mailings, you may want to retype your manuscript. It may be salvaged by ironing. Don't laugh. I've ironed many a one to crisp fresh perfection. But if ironing won't make it look "just typed," then it will be worth your time to retype it.

7. Schedule your writing.

The following calendar will help in this area. Editors welcome work that arrives far enough in advance that they can plan to use it in their upcoming seasonal issues (usually six-months-advance planning). Many times, you will get a manuscript back because editors are simply not thinking in those terms yet. Their minds are concerned with the issues at hand. So try to work on their calendar schedule.

This lists most of the major days and events of the year. Add to it as you discover things you are especially interested in.

SUBMIT

January

Fourth of July
Baseball and other summer
   sports

SUBMIT

July

New Year's Day
Jackson Day
First Shot in Civil War, 1861

Outdoor safety: sunburn,
   bites, traffic

February

Touring
Camping
Fishing
Mountains
Beach resorts
Outdoor fun

March

Labor Day
Swimming
Picnics; Boating
Vacations

April

Columbus Day
Navy Day
Halloween
Indian Summer themes

May

Harvest
Thanksgiving
Election Day; Armistice Day
National Book Week
American Education Week
Football

June

Christmas
Winter sports
Attack on Pearl Harbor
Boston Tea Party, 1773
Slavery abolished in the
   United States, 1865
First successful airplane
   flight, 1903

Winter sports: skiing,
   sledding, et cetera.

August

Candlemas Day
Boy Scouts Anniversary
   (1910)
Lincoln's Birthday
Valentine's Day
Washington's Birthday

September

Pre-spring themes
Indoor sports

October

Good Friday
Easter
Flowers
April Fool's Day

November

Spring themes, love, romance
Gardening
House repairs
May Day; Child Health Week
Mother's Day; Derby Day
National Music Week

December

Weddings; June brides
Summer sports
Flag Day
Father's Day
D-Day, 1944

8. Choose what copyrights you sell.

Everything you write has many publication rights. In the beginning, you may want to abide by the editor's publishing policy. Most of them are fair. But you should be aware that many magazines purchase "all rights" and their check in payment for your manuscript will so state. But you should decide if you want to sell "all rights" of the piece.

In every sentence you write, these copyrights are available:

1. First North American Serial rights.
2. Second North American Serial rights (magazine reprint).
3. Syndicate rights.
4. Foreign rights.
5. Book rights.
6. Book Reprint rights.
7. Dramatization rights (radio, stage, TV, movie).

If you want to retain rights to an article, short story, or poem, you should write on the bottom of the last page of the manuscript this desire: First rights only. Then after publication, you may submit the manuscript to another magazine with the notation that you are selling: Second rights only.

Those publishing companies who purchase only "all rights" may not be interested in "hassling" if you seek to sell "first rights only." They have to want a manuscript pretty badly to go to the trouble of writing a special clause on the purchase order. So, while still an "unknown," you may want to consider that. Usually a company that purchases all rights will be willing to reassign the other rights to you after publication if you make a written request.

9. Never submit a manuscript to more than one editor at a time.

The only time when this does not hold true is in regard to a syndicated newspaper column. You may go to the Directory of Newspapers in your local library and send your proposal for a column with written samples to every city and town on the same day. The only ethical rule here is that you do not send to more than one newspaper in the same city or town.

10. Keep a copy.

Manuscripts do get lost in the mails. Always make a carbon of everything you write.

11. Don't stuff an envelope.

Manuscripts less than six pages should be folded like a business letter and mailed in a ⅹ10 envelope.

Manuscripts seven to ten pages in length may be folded in the middle and mailed in six-by-nine envelopes.

Manuscripts more than ten pages in length should be mailed flat in nine-by-twelve manila envelopes.

12. Keep records of location and date of sending each manuscript.

Every writer probably has his own system. Mine is that I have numbered all of the editors with whom I work in alphabetical order like this: Top of the Page: A

1.   Abingdon Press. Address. Any other information I want there.

2.   Appleton-Century-Crofts. . . .

In a notebook, I write the name of a manuscript after which I make this entry (A-1; 3/20). That tells me that I mailed that piece to Abingdon Press on March 20. If it is returned, I may make the next entry (A-2; 4/1) indicating that I mailed the same piece to Appleton-Century-Crofts on April 1. This is an easy effective system.

13. Keep in touch with manuscripts.

If you have not heard from the publisher in six to eight weeks, you should write to ask if the manuscript was received. Be courteous and tell the editor he may keep it for further study, if so desired, but you would like to be apprised of whether or not the piece was in his possession or had been lost in the mails.

To help build your list of editors, you may want to check the book *The Writer's Market,* which is published each year with the most current information. This is available at your local library for reference. If you would like to own a copy, it may be ordered by writing to the Writer's Digest, 9933 Alliance Road, Cincinnati, Ohio 45242.

THE CONCLUDING PRAYER

Lord . . .
Bless this task . . .
Bless this writing creatively task . . .
> Techniques to be learned
> Manuscripts to be written
> Discipline to be attained

Bless this task . . .
And me
> As I proceed to tackle it.

Lord . . .
Bless my mind . . .
Bless my creative challenging mind . . .
> Cluttered and cobwebby
> Catchall for outgrown opinions and ill-fitting prejudices
> Compartments of clichés that need a good airing.

Bless my mind . . .
And me
> As I proceed to use it.

Lord . . .
Bless my life . . .

Bless my unintentionally haphazard life . . .
    Help me to think with lucidity
    Help me to act with integrity
    Help me to record my creations with best efforts
Bless my life . . .
And me
    As I proceed to develop it.
    This is my prayer today . . .
    Unorthodox, perhaps,
    But the honest outreach
    Of an inquiring mind
        a God-given life-venture
        a longing-to-share spirit.
Lord . . .
Bless this task . . .
                and me . . .
                        as I proceed to achieve it.
                                    Amen.